To

HARRY A. MILLIS

Patterns of
UNION-MANAGEMENT RELATIONS

United Automobile Workers (CIO) • General Motors • Studebaker

by
FREDERICK H. HARBISON
Associate Professor of Economics
The University of Chicago

and

ROBERT DUBIN
Assistant Professor of Industrial Relations
The University of Chicago

↑ 935751

SPINDLETOP ENGINEERING LIBRARY
LAMAR STATE COLLEGE OF TECHNOLOGY

SCIENCE RESEARCH ASSOCIATES, CHICAGO, 1947

COPYRIGHT 1947 BY INDUSTRIAL RELATIONS CENTER
THE UNIVERSITY OF CHICAGO

ALL RIGHTS RESERVED UNDER FOURTH INTERNATIONAL
AMERICAN CONVENTION (1910)

PRINTED IN THE UNITED STATES OF AMERICA

This book may not be reproduced, in whole or in part, in any form (except by reviewers for the public press) without written permission from the publishers.

Patterns of Union-Management Relations

SRA INDUSTRIAL RELATIONS SERIES

The following books are published for the Industrial Relations Center of the University of Chicago

Harbison and Dubin, *Patterns of Union-Management Relations*
Gomberg, *A Trade Union Analysis of Time Study*

INDUSTRIAL RELATIONS CENTER
THE UNIVERSITY OF CHICAGO

Robert Kenneth Burns, *Executive Officer*
Frederick Harris Harbison, *Executive Officer*
Harry Alvin Millis, *Senior Advisor*
Robert Dubin, *Manager*
Arthur Carstens, *Director of Union Programs*
William Lloyd Warner, *Chairman, Committee on Human Relations in Industry*
William Foote Whyte, *Executive Secretary, Committee on Human Relations in Industry*

FACULTY PANEL

Garfield V. Cox, Ph.D., *Dean of the School of Business*
Cyril Orvin Houle, Ph.D., *Dean of University College*
Ralph Winfred Tyler, Ph.D., *Chairman of the Department of Education and University Examiner*
Theodore William Schultz, Ph.D., *Chairman of the Department of Economics and Professor of Agricultural Economics*
William Fielding Ogburn, Ph.D., LL.D., *Distinguished Service Professor of Sociology*
Leonard Dupee White, Ph.D., *Chairman of the Administrative Committee of the Department of Political Science and Professor of Public Administration*
Paul Howard Douglas, Ph.D., *Professor of Economics*
Charles Oscar Gregory, A.B., LL.B., *Professor of Law*
Raleigh Webster Stone, Ph.D., *Professor of Industrial Relations*
William Lloyd Warner, A.B., *Professor of Anthropology and Sociology and Chairman, Committee on Human Relations in Industry*
Louis Wirth, Ph.D., *Professor of Sociology*
Robert Kenneth Burns, Ph.D., *Associate Professor of Social Science*
Frederick Harris Harbison, Ph.D., *Associate Profesor of Economics*
Everett Cherrington Hughes, Ph.D., *Associate Professor of Sociology*
William Foote Whyte, Ph.D., *Associate Professor of Sociology*
Robert Dubin, Ph.D., *Assistant Professor of Industrial Relations*
Avery Leiserson, Ph.D., *Assistant Professor of Political Science*
Joel Seidman, *Assistant Professor of Social Science*
Robert Tannenbaum, M.B.A., *Assistant Professor of Industrial Relations*
Arthur Carstens, A.M., *Lecturer in University College and Director of Union Programs, Industrial Relations Center*

Foreword

THIS IS one of a series of major studies in industrial relations being undertaken at the University of Chicago.

Various members of the faculty and staff of the University who are associated with the Industrial Relations Center are carrying forward research in many areas of industrial relations, including union-management relations, the theory of wages, financial and non-financial incentives, the law of labor, human problems of industrial organization, the relation of industry to the community, and educational methods for union and management personnel.

This volume falls within the area of union-management relations. During the past year an attempt has been made to develop a new framework for the analysis of labor relations. The first application of this framework is set forth in these two studies.

This book is a joint undertaking. Mr. Harbison is responsible for Part II, "General Motors and the UAW"; Mr. Dubin is responsible for Part III, "Studebaker and the UAW." Part I, "Introduction," and Part IV, "Conclusions," were developed jointly.

Executives of the General Motors Corporation and the Studebaker Corporation and local and international officers of the UAW-CIO made many constructive suggestions and expressed critical opinions of individual sections of this book. It is necessary to add that General Motors executives and UAW officials expressed disagreement and alarm at the manner in which the subject matter of Chapter II is presented. Each seemed to feel that "the other side" was treated in too favorable a manner.

Staff members of the Industrial Relations Center and members of the faculty of the University have also contributed valuable comments and criticisms. In particular, we wish to express appreciation to Arthur Carstens, Everett C. Hughes, Avery Leiserson, Harry A. Millis, William H. Nichols, Louis Wirth, and William F. Whyte for critical reading of the manuscript. Special appreciation is due King Carr of the Center's staff for research and editorial assistance. The Social Science Research Committee of the University of Chicago made available the funds necessary for this study. Acknowledgment is made to the following publishers who have generously given permission to quote from their copyrighted works as indicated in the text: John Day Company, Inc., The Macmillan Company, and Yale University Labor and Management Center.

This volume is not in any sense endorsed by the Union or the Corporations. The authors assume full responsibility for it.

ROBERT K. BURNS
FREDERICK H. HARBISON
Executive Officers, Industrial Relations Center

Chicago, Illinois
October, 1947

Contents

Part One: Introduction
 I. Union-Management Relations in Mass Production Industries 3

Part Two: General Motors and the UAW
 II. Corporation and Union Programs and Strategies 15
 III. The Resulting Union-Management Relationship 65

Part Three: Studebaker and the UAW
 IV. Background and Approach to Union-Management Relations 103
 V. Collective Bargaining between Studebaker and Local 5, UAW-CIO . . . 134

Part Four: Conclusions
 VI. Significance of Bigness in Union-Management Relations 181
 VII. The Nature and Scope of Constructive Union-Management Relations 202

Index 225

Introduction

PART ONE

It is plain from the slightest consideration of practical affairs, or the most superficial reading of industrial history, that free competition means combination, and that the organization of the world, now going on so fast, means an ever increasing might and scope of combination. It seems to me futile to set our faces against this tendency. Whether beneficial on the whole, as I think it, or detrimental, it is inevitable, unless the fundamental axioms of society, and even the fundamental conditions of life, are to be changed. . . . . One of the eternal conflicts out of which life is made up is that between the effort of every man to get the most he can for his services, and that of society, disguised under the name of capital, to get his services for the least possible return. Combination on the one side is patent and powerful. Combination on the other is the necessary and desirable counterpart, if the battle is to be carried on in a fair and equal way.—JUSTICE OLIVER WENDELL HOLMES, dissenting in *Vegelahn* v. *Guntner,* 1896.

CHAPTER I

Union-Management Relations in Mass Production Industries

THE impact of powerful labor unions on the business enterprise system has caused great changes in the American economy during the past decade. Prior to the depression of the thirties, business enterprise was the principal force shaping the social and political life of the nation. But the era of unchallenged leadership of business, which probably reached its peak in the twenties, has passed. Today, labor unions, particularly those operating in basic industries, have acquired economic and political strength which matches at many points the power and influence possessed by business organizations.

The competition for leadership between business and unions at times has resulted in open conflict and nation-wide strikes in the basic industries. Consequently, by 1947 the "labor problem" had become perhaps the most crucial domestic issue facing the nation.

An underlying purpose of research in labor-management relations should be to analyze the impact of labor unions on the business enterprise system. This calls for an objective appraisal of the nature of the various kinds of relationships between unions and employers and an understanding of the influence which such relationships have on the nation's economic, social and political institutions. It also calls, we feel, for a completely new approach to the study of the "labor problem."

Obviously, labor-management relations should be studied within the context of the basic characteristics of the modern business enterprise system and the present-day union movement in America. It is appropriate, therefore, to set forth at this point our concept of the significant features and developing trends which characterize business and unions.

The American business enterprise system is not and never has been a completely free competitive system; yet it is not a monopolistic system. It is a mixture of competition and monopoly. It is a system which has been largely successful in producing the goods and services which our society demands. America, operating under this system, has achieved the highest standard of living in the world. Nevertheless, our present economic organization has not achieved stability and freedom from alternating cycles of prosperity and depression.

The concentration of economic power in large corporations is one of the significant characteristics of our business enterprise system. As Berle and Means pointed out over ten years ago, it is necessary to think of the enterprise system in terms of the far-reaching influence of large corporate units rather than in terms of a multitude of small competing firms. In concluding a chapter on the "Concentration of Economic Power," Berle and Means stated:

> A society in which production is governed by blind economic forces is being replaced by one in which production is being carried on under the ultimate control of a handful of individuals. The economic power in the hands of the few persons who control a giant corporation is a tremendous force which can harm or benefit a multitude of individuals, affect whole districts, shift the currents of trade, bring ruin to one community and prosperity to another. The organizations which they control have passed far beyond the realm of private enterprise—they have become more nearly social institutions.

Such is the character of the corporate system—dynamic, constantly building itself into greater aggregates, and thereby changing the basic conditions which the thinking of the past has assumed.[1]

There have been indications, furthermore, that the trend is in the direction of even greater concentration of economic power in large groups.[2]

In the mass production industries corporations such as General Motors, United States Steel, and General Electric represent concentrations of economic power which put them in an influential position of leadership in their respective industries. Because of their size, prestige, and position of leadership, these corporations have carried considerable weight in the affairs of government at the local, state, and federal levels. They also have had a far-reaching influence on the social institutions in the communities in which their many plants are located.

Traditionally, the smaller concerns in these industries have operated within an economic environment created to a great extent by the larger units. The smaller units have usually been free to compete among themselves and with the big corporations. In fact, in many

---

[1] A. A. Berle and Gardner C. Means, *The Modern Corporation and Private Property* (New York: The Macmillan Co., 1936), p. 46.

[2] Berle and Means in their study concluded that, on the basis of gross assets, the large corporations were growing two or three times as fast as other corporations in the non-financial group. *Ibid.,* p. 40.

The Smaller War Plants Corporation in its report, *Economic Concentration and World War II,* presents a more recent summary on the general topic of economic concentration. The report indicates that, after a reversal in the early thirties, the trend observed by Berle and Means continued at least up to the time we entered the war. After a careful examination of our wartime economy, the report concluded that "the relative importance of big business, particularly the giant corporations, increased sharply during the war." Looking further into the character of the economy on V-J Day, the report indicated that "economic concentration will probably be higher in the postwar years than before the war." U.S. Congress, Senate, *Economic Concentration and World War II:* Report of the Smaller War Plants Corporation to the Special Committee to Study Problems of American Small Business (Washington, D.C.: Government Printing Office, 1946), pp. 6–7, 21–54, 55–64.

cases they have been better managed than the large corporations and have taken business away from their more powerful competitors. Yet, for the most part, they have sold in markets influenced primarily by the policies and actions of the big corporations rather than by purely competitive economic forces. The most successful smaller enterprises have usually been those which have made the most fortunate or far-sighted adjustment to this kind of economic environment.

Paralleling the system of business enterprise is the system of organized labor which we term the "union movement." It first emerged as a really permanent and powerful force in the economy during the thirties. Particularly in the vital basic industries, the union movement is new and has grown very rapidly. For this reason it is perhaps neither as widely accepted nor as generally understood as the business enterprise system.

The labor organizations which make up the union movement have directly or indirectly affected the thinking and actions of practically all employers, organized or unorganized. In the organized plants there is formal bargaining between unions and employers. Employers who are not organized usually try to match or better the conditions in the organized plants in order to "make a union unnecessary" in their own establishments. Consequently, union pressures are felt generally throughout business.

The union movement is a mixture of large and small labor organizations with widely differing objectives, policies and leadership. There is not now nor has there ever been a unified labor movement in this country. There is the obvious split between the American Federation of Labor and the Congress of Industrial Organizations; there are the less obvious but often more bitter cleavages between the unions within these camps. There are jurisdictional disputes and ideological controversies. The policies and practices of locals and their international unions, as well as internal politics and controls vary widely. American business leaders have no monopoly on the spirit of rugged individualism and independent thinking. After all, the AFL has been organized on the basis of maintenance and protection of the individual interests and jurisdictions of its member unions. The CIO has also been organized on the basis of safeguarding the autonomy of its constituent organizations. In many respects the American union movement is a sort of competitive system within itself.

In the union movement, as in the business enterprise system, however, there is a high degree of concentration of economic and political power in the hands of those who lead the large organizations. Unions like the United Steelworkers, the United Automobile Workers, and the United Mine Workers and a half a dozen others each have hundreds of thousands of members. When the leaders of these unions bargain with the employers in basic industries, they determine the wages, working conditions and general economic welfare of millions of workers. The smaller unions in closely related or allied industries for the most part must operate within the limits of economic concessions which these big unions secure, mostly in bargaining with the large employers. In some cases the smaller labor organizations or independent unions may follow the patterns set by the big unions; in some cases they may be able to better the pattern; in others they may fall short of it. But by and large the smaller unions operate with reference to the precedents established by the powerful international unions which possess the most effective economic and political power in the labor movement.

If the objective of research in labor-management relations is to analyze the impact of the union movement on the business enterprise system, then the logical first step is to observe the interactions between the two systems at the point where power concentrations on both sides are the greatest. Probably the most important "power points" of this kind are to be found in the basic industries. Corporations such as General Motors, United States Steel, and General Electric stand face to face with labor unions such as the United Automobile Workers, the United Steelworkers, and the United Electrical Radio and Machine Workers. The relationships between such big corporations and unions have brought into existence new power structures which are having a tremendous influence in the economy and in the social and political life of the nation. Yet relatively little is known about the nature and consequence of big-league labor-management relationships of this kind.

Outside the scope of the mass production industries there are many union-management relationships which often follow individual courses. For example, in the building trades, the printing industry and local service industries, collective bargaining is carried on in a more traditional sense, outside the general influence of union-management relations in the mass production industries. The older order of unionism still exists as an important foundation for the newer unionism. However, we are concerned in this book with the influence of the unions in the mass production industries and we have directed our attention primarily at the automotive industry.

From the automotive industry we have selected two significant points of interaction between the union movement and the business enterprise system. The first study deals with the relationship between the UAW-CIO and General Motors Corporation from 1936 to 1947. It is an example of what we call a "labor-management power center" where concentrated power on the side of industry meets concentrated power on the side of labor. The second study outlines the relationship between the Studebaker Corporation and a local union of the UAW-CIO. It illustrates one kind of adjustment, and a very constructive adjustment, which a smaller company and a local union can make as they bargain in the shadow of the giants of the industry.

In the General Motors case we have focused attention on these questions: What is the influence of the size of companies and unions on the labor-management relations which exist between them? To what extent do the relations between big corporations and big unions depend upon political as well as economic factors? What is the basis for the apparent predominance of conflict in relationships between labor and management in the power centers? Can the issues in these power centers be resolved by so-called free collective bargaining? Can relationships between the big corporations and unions be looked upon as the private affairs of the parties involved? Finally, what are the actual and possible effects of bigness in labor-management relations on the economic, social, and political structure of the nation?

In the Studebaker case we have raised these questions: What were the forces which led to the initial rapprochement of management and union in the development of constructive union-management relations? What influence does the collective bargaining pattern established at a labor-management power center have on labor-management relations in a pattern-adjusting situation like that at Studebaker? In what respects is the pattern not followed? What is the characteristic way in which collective bargaining is carried out in a constructive union-management relationship? In such a relationship, how secure is the union with respect to management, its members, and the community in which it operates? What kind of power relations exist between company and union where cooperative elements predominate in their dealings with each other? What are the attitudes of interaction between company and union which practical management and union officials develop to make constructive relations a reality?

The General Motors situation is illustrative of labor relations at one of the power centers of the automotive industry. There is reason to believe, on the basis of general observations, that comparable labor-management power centers in industries such as steel, electrical manufacturing, meat packing, and others have many of the same characteristics set forth in the General Motors case. The existence of union-management power centers makes the economy increasingly dependent upon intelligent and realistic exercise of influence and authority by a relatively small group of company executives and labor officials who hold positions of responsibility in the big corporations and unions. The consequences of their actions are so far-reaching that collective bargaining between these unions and corporations is now a matter of primary public concern.

The Studebaker case represents a constructive type of labor relations which is developing largely in the smaller units of the mass production industries. In preliminary studies we have found parallel examples of truly constructive relations in steel, automotive parts, metal fabricating and processing, electrical manufacture and meat packing. On the other hand, this constructive type of relationship is at present the exception rather than the rule in mass production industries. In these industries there are instances where the parties have not achieved anything approaching the stable and mutually satisfactory relationship found at Studebaker. In a great many of these cases the pattern of conflict so often apparent in the power centers is reflected or even magnified in the union-management relationships dependent upon such centers.

A comprehensive study of the pattern of labor relations in mass production industries would necessarily require an analysis of many different union-management types and their relationship one to another. It would require consideration of the possible shifting of pattern-setting functions between various power centers in an industry (such as, for example, from General Motors to Ford or Chrysler). It would also raise the crucial question of the inter-relationship between power centers of different industries (such as the influence of the decisions made in United States Steel on those made in General Motors, General Electric, etc.). These vital considerations lie beyond the scope of this volume.

Our study of General Motors and Studebaker suggests that there is no such thing as a single "labor problem" in America. It demonstrates that there is no prototype of labor-management relationship in the mass production industries. It shows that there is no single concept of what collective bargaining is, its area, scope, or appropriate function. If the term "collective bargaining" is used to describe what transpires between the Studebaker Corporation and Local 5 of the UAW, then a different term should be coined to designate the relationship between General Motors and the top command of the same union. The Studebaker case compares with General Motors in somewhat the same sense as an individual warship compares with a naval task force.

However, the assumption that each individual labor-management relationship is unique seems hardly warranted. In practice, although there are differences in labor-management types, these types are usually closely inter-related in recognizable patterns. Certainly, this is true of General Motors and Studebaker. It is very important, therefore, to observe the manner in which labor-management types are related to each other, thus forming patterns of labor relations in mass production industries.

The findings based upon research of this kind may lead, we hope, to a more precise understanding of the nature and consequences of labor relations throughout the country as a whole and in the mass production industries in particular. This volume represents only a modest first step toward this goal.

General Motors and the UAW

PART TWO

CHAPTER II

Corporation and Union Programs and Strategies

IN FINANCIAL resources, technological development, and sales, General Motors is one of the largest corporations in the world. It is clearly the leader of the automotive industry since it makes nearly half of the passenger cars and trucks produced in this country. It is also a major manufacturer of diesel-electric railway locomotives, refrigeration and air-conditioning equipment, heating equipment, electric ranges, home lighting and water systems, and a host of related products. In 1947 it employed nearly 300,000 workers in 117 plants in this country alone, and had more than 450,000 stockholders.

From any point of view, General Motors is big. It directly affects the lives of hundreds of thousands of workers. It plays an important role in the communities where its plants are located. The thinking and actions of its management directly or indirectly affect the lives of millions of individuals. It holds a position of influence and leadership in the economic and political life of the nation which goes far beyond the confines of the automotive industry. It is not surprising, therefore, that General Motors has long been recognized by a large segment of American industry as a pattern-setter in the field of labor relations.

In 1947 General Motors had bargaining relationships with twenty-eight different international unions and had in force eighty-five separate agreements with labor organizations. A large majority of its workers are represented by the United Automobile, Aircraft and Agricultural Implement Workers (UAW-CIO). For many years General Motors' dealings with organized labor have hinged primarily on its relationship with this one union. The UAW represented approximately 270,000 GM workers in March, 1947. At that time the total number of workers represented by the UAW which included aircraft, farm implement, and other industrial workers was well over one million. Actual membership of UAW rose to a peak of over a million in 1943, fell off during reconversion, and climbed to about 900,000 in March, 1947. The UAW then had contracts in 124 separate bargaining units of the corporation in fifty cities in the United States and Canada.[1]

The UAW-CIO, which represents approximately 90 per cent of the corporation's hourly rated workers in the automobile and auto parts operations, is one of the most powerful unions in the nation. The General Motors local unions in UAW constituted about one-third of the union's membership. Under the leadership of Walter P. Reuther the UAW has concentrated its bargaining strategy on its relations with General Motors. The influence of the union, like that of the corporation, extends far beyond the automotive industry. The UAW is a major force in the community life of scores of automobile plant cities. At times it has wielded tremendous influence in national affairs. Through collective bargaining and political action it has had a very real effect on the lives of millions of workers and citizens.

---

[1] Other unions in the industry (mainly International Association of Machinists; Mechanics Education Society) and in General Motors outside auto and auto parts (e.g. United Electrical Workers) have a lesser influence on GM contract clauses.

Consequently, the labor-management relationship at General Motors has been characterized by concentrations of economic and political power which generate collective bargaining decisions and economic patterns that reverberate throughout the economy.

General Motors, like other large corporations in the mass production industries, was an open shop stronghold until the advent of the New Deal. By one means or another the corporation had not only discouraged but on occasion had vigorously suppressed union organization in its plants. The unions which attempted to organize General Motors in the early years had, for the most part, shown themselves to be incapable in leadership, financial resources and structure, of organizing mass production workers. Yet almost overnight in 1937 General Motors was unionized, and since has been one of the strategic bases for the spread of unionism throughout the country. General Motors became a union stronghold of the first order.

REASONS WHY GENERAL MOTORS WAS UNIONIZED

Why was General Motors organized? As one might expect, this question has been answered in different ways by persons on opposite sides of the fence, as well as by many observers sitting on the fence. A majority agree, however, that most of the reasons were in one way or another related to the following factors: (1) the insecurity of workers—aggravated by the depression; (2) the pent-up resentment of many workers with the manner in which available jobs were controlled by management coupled with a feeling among employees that they had no place to go for protection; and (3) a governmental policy that encouraged unionization and collective bargaining. Had any one of these conditions been absent, it is unlikely that General Motors and, for that matter, most other mass production corporations, would have been organized during the thirties. What has been the background related to these three factors?

The automotive industry has always been susceptible to cyclical fluctuations in market demand. During depressions old cars are "made to last longer" and few new buyers appear on the market. Both the demand for replacements and the demand from new buyers on which auto production schedules depend fall off rapidly and the curtailed production is reflected in unemployment and competition among workers for the few remaining jobs. Employment in the automotive industry fell 75 per cent from 1929 to 1932, a larger decrease than the average for the national economy as a whole.

In addition, traditional lay-offs of production workers each year during the period of retooling and change-over to new models increased workers' uncertainty and job insecurity. Although by 1936 there had been substantial business recovery, the volume of unemployment was still high, and those who were returning to work were bitter over the hardships they had experienced in the previous depression years. Auto workers were ready to support a plan or program which held out some hope for achieving job security.

During this depression period many workers had intense resentment against management methods of "big business." Jobs were scarce and the employer controlled them. Job tenure too often depended upon nepotism and favoritism. Workers who kept on good terms with their foremen were thought to get the breaks. There was also widespread dissatisfaction over the setting of production standards and the speed of production lines. Workers recognized that the employers could easily find replacements for those who were not willing to comply with company standards. This aggravated employees' feelings of fear and insecurity. They were naturally sympathetic, in many cases, to a union which promised to take job control out of the hands of management.

The final factor was the government policy under the New Deal of encouraging unionization. As part of a program to aid economic recovery, government policy and legislation gave protection to workers' rights to organize into unions and to bargain collectively through representatives of their own choice. The intent of Section 7a of the National Industrial Recovery Act of 1933, and of the Wagner Act of 1935, was to encourage the growth of unions by making it illegal for employers to interfere with them. The New Deal legislation provided both a legal and publicly receptive environment which made it possible for union leaders to organize traditionally open-shop mass production industries.

THE YEARS OF UPHEAVAL: 1937–1940

In General Motors the transition to unionization and collective bargaining was turbulent and violent. The UAW-CIO established itself in General Motors by means of the sit-down strikes in 1936–37. A small group of militant workers and union leaders shut down a few key plants which were the nerve centers of General Motors. This group demanded, as the price for giving "possession" of the plants back to management, recognition of the union and the inauguration of collective bargaining on seniority rights, grievance procedure, and joint regulation of the speed of production lines. General Motors instituted injunction proceedings against the sit-downers and did its best to organize public opinion against the strikers. But the sit-downers held fast. The Governor of Michigan, who wanted the strike settled as rapidly as possible, put pressure on the corporation to make an agreement with the union. On February 11, 1937, General Motors agreed to recognize the UAW as the bargaining agent for those employees who were union members and to negotiate with the union over other unsettled issues.

The UAW consolidated its victory by conducting an intensive organization drive among General Motors workers. Having a firm foothold in General Motors, the UAW was able to organize rapidly the other automobile corporations (with the exception of Ford), as well as most of the parts and accessory manufacturers in and near the auto centers. Most of the industry had stood behind General Motors in opposing unions. In 1937 the industry was obliged to conform to the pattern of recognizing and dealing with them.

The attitudes and feelings of the parties as they embarked upon their new relationship were of great importance. In the minds of the sit-down strikers and union leaders, a victory had been won over a corporation whose objective, they firmly believed, was the exploitation of workers, a corporation which had used spies and strong arm tactics to suppress the workers' fight for security and a decent standard of living—a "monopoly" with an "insatiable greed for profits" and an "arrogant disregard for the public interest." It is important to bear in mind that the union looked upon itself as a protest organization which had wrested recognition from a corporation that fought unions for years.[2]

On the corporation side there was also a feeling of bitterness and resentment toward the union leaders. Man-

---

[2] Walter Reuther has stated, for example, that the UAW was built up against great opposition from the auto companies who resorted to "the most vicious brutality, with the employment of underworld thugs and gangsters and spies and the expenditures of millions of dollars in the most vicious anti-American campaign conceivable."

agement believed that the seizure of its plants was communist-inspired. It disliked intensely the apparent sympathy and backing which union agitators (who, they claimed, had resorted to violence and illegal seizure of company property) got from a "leftish" government. It resented the disrespect for discipline and authority on the part of union trouble-makers. It was forced to bargain with a militant labor organization whose avowed purpose was to challenge, if not to undermine, management's position of leadership.

Unlike the parallel case of the United States Steel Corporation, union-management relations at General Motors did not start with a voluntary peace pact or compromise. They were born out of strife and violence on a battleground where neither side offered nor expected any quarter. Although the conflict between General Motors and the UAW-CIO was much more civilized by 1947 than ten years before, the suspicion, resentment, and distrust of each side for the other still prevailed. In short, the scars of the early conflict were plainly visible in spite of a decade of collective bargaining.

The early development of collective bargaining in the automotive industry and in General Motors was complicated by intense internal factional differences in the union. Out of the grass-roots militancy of the virtually autonomous local unions in Cleveland, Detroit, Flint, and other centers of the automotive industry grew bitter rivalries over programs, leadership, and power in the International Union. There were purges, "hatchet jobs," trials and villifications which were climaxed by the ousting of the union president, Homer Martin, in 1939. This climactic blow split the union wide open.

R. J. Thomas, formerly vice-president under Homer Martin, was elected international president of the UAW-CIO in 1939. Homer Martin became president of a rival

AFL auto workers' union. The ensuing contest between the two unions almost destroyed the union organization in most of the General Motors plants.

The corporation refused to bargain with either organization until a determination could be made as to which was to have exclusive bargaining status in the various plants. At this point the UAW-CIO under the leadership of Walter P. Reuther, director of the union's General Motors Department, engineered the "Strategy Strike of 1939" to establish the position of the CIO union in General Motors and to wipe out Martin's AFL group. While General Motors was tooling up for 1940 models, the UAW-CIO struck the tool and die shops, where it had its only effective concentration of strength. The tool and die workers in twelve of General Motors' shops refused to complete their work on the 1940 models until the corporation recognized the UAW-CIO. By this tactic the CIO group in effect re-won recognition in forty-two General Motors plants. In the subsequent National Labor Relations Board elections of April, 1940, the UAW-CIO won substantial majorities of plant workers in forty-nine General Motors plants. For the first time it was recognized as the exclusive bargaining agent, not just for union members but for all production and maintenance workers in the bargaining units in which it had won elections. The UAW-CIO victory in the NLRB elections marked the beginning of corporation-wide bargaining at General Motors. The AFL group had been eliminated from most of the plants. The UAW-CIO's GM Department took over as the coordinating body of the union's struggle with the corporation.

The immediate effect of union organization on the corporation was to bring into sharp focus some basic management weaknesses in industrial relations. Although the top executives knew something of the abuses inherent in the methods of wage payment, the lay-off and recall procedure, and the system of handling worker grievances, they seemed largely unaware of the intense resentment then existing in the plants. Before the appearance of the union, lines of communications with workers had been largely downward. After the union became established the pressures of communication were upward. It became apparent to top management that there were many causes of worker resentment to be eliminated.

An even greater management weakness was the inexperience and lack of training of the supervisory forces in the handling of human relations. The advent of the union tended to shatter the morale of many company foremen. The UAW, bursting with energy and fired by struggles for power between rival factions, ran wild in many plants for months after the original agreements were signed. In effect a rebellion occurred against managerial discipline in many of the shops. The newly elected union committeemen were "biting at the heels of the foremen" with all sorts of beefs, complaints, grievances, and outright threats. Where this kind of direct action brought no results, sit-down strikes and "quickies" were organized. Many of the local plant managements simply lacked the know-how to cope with the situation. To make matters worse, some of the foremen were completely intimidated by the union.

Obviously, General Motors needed to build an organization to formulate labor policies and administer them on all levels. It was faced also with the task of training thousands of foremen, supervisors, and plant managers in the techniques of personnel management and relations with the union. Above all, it was necessary to bolster the morale of supervisory forces by backing them up on matters involving shop discipline. The top executives recognized these things would have to be done—and done quickly—to prevent the union from "taking over" in the shops.

We have skipped rapidly over the early years of bargaining prior to 1940. It was a turbulent period during which both the corporation and the union struggled to consolidate their respective organizations. Both sides were formulating policies and strategies for dealing with each other. It was a period of adjustment when the actions and decisions made by both parties were to all outward appearances in a state of flux. Both sides were inexperienced in collective bargaining and were faced with very pressing problems of internal organization.

In these first years of its mushroom growth the demands of the UAW were traditional: job security through stricter application of seniority,[3] higher pay, better conditions in the shops, an opportunity to limit the authority of the foreman. In this period local union leaders pulled "quickies" and sit-downs as a means of pressing local grievances and demonstrating their newly won "freedom" from the authority of management. The program of the union was decentralized for the most part. Each local fought for its own survival and bargained with local plant management. The energies of the union were directed almost entirely toward establishment of recognition and bargaining on wages, hours and conditions of employment, while it was struggling with internal factional disputes.

During the same period the corporation was pre-

---

[3] For some time prior to the advent of the UAW, General Motors had applied, with qualifications, the seniority principle in lay-offs and rehiring. It retained considerable discretion, however, in making exceptions in the application of the principle on the basis of skill and ability. The union pressed for straight seniority, attempting to minimize any deviation from length of service on the basis of skill and ability. It also wanted to make seniority a matter of right as defined in union-management contracts, and thus wanted to wrest control from the automotive companies over the manner in which the seniority principle was applied.

paring itself to administer a labor relations policy throughout its far-flung organization. At the outset, its industrial relations organization contained only a handful of executives in the Detroit office of the corporation and a series of employment offices in its various manufacturing divisions. By 1947 there were a large number of trained industrial relations experts in the Detroit office. Labor relations had become a top management function. In each major manufacturing division there was a personnel department responsible for the coordination of labor relations and broad industrial relations programs at the plant level. In terms of breadth of activities and numbers of persons engaged in industrial relations work, only two or three corporations could match the General Motors setup.

Since 1940 there has been evidence on both sides of the development of consistent policies, programs, and strategies. By 1947 there was abundant evidence of firmly rooted beliefs and ideologies held by officials in both camps. As a result, the aims and objectives of both the corporation and the union were quite clear cut and logical. This relationship between the UAW-CIO and General Motors poses many vital questions essential to an understanding of collective bargaining between big corporations and big unions.

What have been the motivations, policies, and goals of the respective parties in this relationship? How have policy decisions been made by the corporation and the union? In what areas and to what extent have the ideologies, beliefs, and programs of the parties been in conflict with one another? In what areas have the parties developed an effective system for solving problems jointly? What prognosis can be offered for this labor-management relationship? What are its implications for the economy?

THE UNION FACES THE CORPORATION

The UAW-CIO concept—particularly that of the Reuther group—of the functions and problems of collective bargaining, as well as its long-range programs and objectives, will be described here. Our purpose is to analyze the structure of beliefs, attitudes, and reactions of the union leadership in General Motors in order to have a better understanding of the part it plays in the labor-management relationship.

The Reuther Group and General Motors

As soon as the UAW-CIO emerged victorious over the Martin forces in the NLRB elections of 1940, new factional coalitions quickly developed. Since that time the struggle for power within the UAW-CIO has raged between the Reuther supporters and various groups which have formed an opposition faction. In the main, this opposition faction has been composed of supporters of George Addes, who became secretary-treasurer of the International Union in 1940. In this faction are found the chief followers of the Communist party line, who have constituted a small but vocal group, and a number of other anti-Reuther groups. The rivalry between factions in the UAW, always bitter and intense, has been aggravated by the fact that the convention strength of both factions has been fairly evenly matched. It has been this situation which has made the UAW-CIO a very unstable organization, but, at the same time, has explained in part its great vitality and militant spirit.

The subject of factionalism within the UAW has been looked upon as a sort of whipping post by the union's opponents, as an example of democracy in action by some of its friends, and as organizational chaos by a good many outsiders who have been unable to understand the complex nature of UAW politics.

In General Motors plants in 1947 the Reuther supporters were clearly dominant, having control over the vast majority of workers under contract with the UAW. Furthermore, the GM Department of the union—the focal point of collective bargaining with the corporation—was pretty solidly in the Reuther camp. Because of the size and prestige of General Motors and the function it has always performed in setting patterns followed by other companies, the Reuther forces, in effect, have thus controlled the keystone of union power in the automotive industry. They have held this strategic position continuously since 1940. Consequently, a description of UAW policy and strategy as it applies to General Motors is in large measure a description of the program of the Reuther group within the union.

Concept of the Function of Collective Bargaining

The UAW won union recognition only after a bitter strike, and later continued to meet with stiff resistance on nearly all of the demands it presented to General Motors. Well aware of the "tough" attitude of General Motors in collective bargaining, the UAW soon recognized that it must stand ready to fight for every improvement it sought to gain in contract negotiations. The corporation has tried to restrict the scope of the collective bargaining relationship while the UAW has fought to expand it. The corporation has wanted to adhere rigidly to the stated provisions of the contract; the union has wanted to stretch the agreement to cover a host of workers' problems which lie outside the area of bargaining as defined in the agreement. The corporation has sought to limit the authority of the impartial umpire; the union has attempted to broaden his functions.

The UAW has pressed for such things as higher wages, more liberal vacations, stricter application of seniority in lay-offs, rehiring and promotion, and improvements in the grievance procedure. It has constantly tried to insure its security by pressing for maintenance of membership and the union shop. It has sought improvements in working conditions and weekly guarantees of employment. These and related issues have fallen within the area of wages, hours and conditions of employment on which the corporation has been willing to bargain with the union, even if it has refused to make the concessions which the union has desired.

The union's concept of the legitimate area of collective bargaining, however, has gone far beyond issues of this nature. It has demanded sick-pay plans and jointly administered pension and retirement programs. It has advocated industry-wide wage equalization and industry-wide collective bargaining in the automotive industry. But General Motors has refused to budge on demands of this type.

For the UAW officials who have dealt with General Motors, collective bargaining has been an arduous day-to-day uphill struggle against a strong and tough opponent. The union, of course, has found the going tougher because it constantly has demanded "more." All unions meet with opposition when they press for wage increases, straight seniority, and other concessions. But unlike some other corporations with which the union has dealt, General Motors has been usually well prepared for negotiations. The union officials responsible for bargaining with the corporation stated when interviewed by the authors that at least they "always know where GM stands."

Most of these officials have believed, however, that General Motors has never genuinely accepted the idea of collective bargaining with bona fide unions. They have felt that the corporation considered the Wagner Act as "temporary legislation" and that it has looked forward to the day when it could "give unions the axe." Although the UAW has developed a fairly satisfactory means of bargaining with the corporation on such matters as individual grievances, seniority, wage levels, and rate structures, its officers were always suspicious of the corporation's "ulterior motives" in its relations with the union. In the minds of nearly every UAW official interviewed there appeared to be stated or implied doubts about the motives of the corporation in collective bargaining. A good many officers, furthermore, seemed to be convinced that General Motors was preparing to bust the union by fair means or foul.

Yet, even without these suspicions and beliefs, the Reuther supporters would not have been content with the "traditional" scope of collective bargaining. They have continued to feel that collective bargaining properly included union participation in the solution of the broad economic problems of the automotive industry, such as the seasonableness and instability of employment and the production, sales, and technological policies of the auto manufacturers. As will be pointed out later, the UAW has been particularly concerned with wage-price relationships not only in the automotive industry but throughout the nation. The UAW idea of collective bargaining has led directly into a concept of industry-wide and nation-wide social and economic planning. Since its pronouncements along this line have been many and spectacular, they deserve careful attention here.

UAW Plans for War Production and Postwar Reconversion

In December, 1940, when the country was experiencing the first jitters of imminent war, Reuther and his followers launched a proposal for converting the unused surplus capacity of the automobile plants to the mass production of war planes.[4] Reuther charged that the auto manufacturers were not facing realistically the task of conversion to defense production. He proposed that the President of the United States appoint a tripartite aviation production board (composed of representatives of industry, labor, and government) with "full authority to organize and supervise the mass production of airplanes in the automobile and auto parts industry." This was the union's first bid for a share in "intelligent planning" and "a voice in matters of policy and administration" in the mass production industries. This proposal was well timed, since it was becoming obvious to many that economic mobilization for war required central planning by the Army, Navy, and civilian production authorities. This plan, which was supported by all groups in the UAW-CIO, was also endorsed by the president of the CIO, and was presented to the appropriate government agencies.[5] This plan along with many other Reuther proposals was widely discussed in government circles, but never adopted as a basic policy in the government's planning of the war production program.

---

[4] Walter P. Reuther, *500 Planes a Day* (Detroit: UAW-CIO Education Dept., 1941). This plan was developed by a committee of auto workers working with Walter Reuther.

[5] The "500 planes a day plan" might be considered as an application of the CIO Industry-Council plan, or the Industry-Council plan might be looked upon as a generalization of the Reuther plan. Nine days before the announcement of the Reuther Plan, Philip Murray, president of the CIO, had released the "CIO Defense Plan," which later, taking the name of its main feature, became known as the "Industry Council Plan." Murray proposed "adequate and centralized planning" of each basic defense industry to insure maximum production. He advocated that labor as a partner in production should share in the planning process. His plan called for the President to establish an Industry Council in each basic defense industry. This Council was to be composed of an equal number of representatives of management and labor in the industry, together with one government representative who was to serve as chairman. The plan also called for the President to create a National Defense Board having the same type of representation, with himself acting as chairman. The National Defense Board

In August, 1941, the UAW called for "all-out" conversion of the industry to war production and gave full backing to those government officials who at that time were advocating drastic curtailment of passenger car production and were meeting with considerable opposition from the automotive industry. By this policy the UAW gained prestige with a great many persons in various government agencies as well as with a large segment of the public.

The automobile manufacturers for their part claimed that the Army, Navy, and War Production Board had no idea of military requirements until well after Pearl Harbor and that, therefore, they were never asked to convert all their facilities to war production. After Pearl Harbor, of course, conversion of the automotive industry to war production became imperative. At a time when the nation was alarmed at the inadequacy of the defense program, the UAW seized the opportunity to charge that the automotive industry was guilty of "providing too little and too late."

During the war the UAW pressed for joint planning and joint advisory committees to guide and administer

---

was to formulate an overall national defense program, the details of which were to be the responsibility of the individual Industry Councils. Specifically, the Industry Council would have had the following duties—in conformance with the policy of, and subject to the review of the National Defense Board:

1. To coordinate the production facilities to meet domestic and armament requirements of the industry with maximum speed, increasing production facilities where necessary.
2. To ascertain the requirements of the industry for men and resources, with the allocation of raw materials, the adjustment of available labor supply, and, when necessary, the training of additional labor in order to achieve maximum production efficiency.
3. To grant and reallocate government contracts in view of the overall industry plan.
4. To promote industrial peace by "the perfection and extension of sound collective bargaining" and by "adherence to all laws affecting the rights and welfare of labor."

the conversion and war production program in the industry. It proposed, first, the pooling of machine tools, critically short at the time, and second, the organization of the entire industry as a single production unit, giving labor along with industry responsibility for broad policy determination. This proposal had a strong appeal to most auto workers and put the union in the position of advocating positive programs for prosecution of the war. Other proposals were presented to government authorities either through labor advisory committees or individual contacts with officials in various agencies.

For the most part, government agencies rejected these proposals for joint committees and joint planning and followed a policy of working with management on all basic production problems. The most that the UAW was able to achieve in joint planning for war production was a government-industry-labor agreement on the seniority status of workers shifting from civilian to war production plants. This deaf-ear treatment was a great disappointment to the UAW-CIO leadership which had hoped to expand its participation in the affairs of the industry to include production planning.

Having been thwarted in their efforts to get joint planning responsibilities in the automotive industry, the UAW leaders next turned their attention to national economic problems. Recognizing that strikes in war industries would be unpopular and might be outlawed, the UAW proposed a voluntary strike moratorium on condition that the government guarantee "equality of sacrifice" on the part of all economic groups in the interest of the war economy. The plan proposed that the government institute rationing and price control, limit war profits to 3 per cent, place a ceiling of $25,000 a year on individual incomes for the duration of the war, and set up a Labor

Production Division in the War Production Board to encourage creative contributions by labor to war production.[6] This program was well timed to appeal to war workers in general and auto workers in particular. It also coincided with measures which the government was instituting then. In response to this and parallel pressures from other sources, price controls and rationing were instituted; a labor production division was set up within the War Production Board; and a surplus war profits taxation program was established. Neither of the latter two programs, however, completely fulfilled the UAW proposals. President Roosevelt advocated the $25,000 limit on individual incomes, but was unable to get acceptance of the proposal by Congress.

From 1943 to 1945 the UAW also pressed its program before the National War Labor Board which, for practical purposes, had the final decision-making power in matters of collective bargaining during the war. In the General Motors case in 1943, the union requested an

---

[6] Walter Reuther, "Equality of Sacrifice," *United Automobile Worker*, April 15, 1942. The "Victory Through Equality of Sacrifice" program, a wartime policy for UAW-CIO, embodied the following points:

1. Corporation profits limited to 3 per cent.
2. Income of individuals or family not to exceed $25,000 annually.
3. Rigid price control to prevent inflation.
4. A fair and just rationing program.
5. Security (guaranteed wage) for dependents of servicemen.
6. A moratorium be declared on all debts during the period of reconversion.
7. A Labor-Production Division be created within the War Production Board.
8. Representatives of labor, government, agriculture, and industry to constitute an agency to plan for peace.
9. On the assurance that the above would become law, the members of the UAW-CIO would take all time over forty hours per week in the form of non-negotiable war bonds.

industry-wide wage stabilization agreement (which was a step in the direction of industry-wide bargaining on wages), a guarantee to every worker of full employment or a guaranteed weekly wage if he should work less than a full week through no fault of his own, a postwar employment security fund, and a wage escalator clause to provide for automatic wage adjustment equal to increases in living costs. At the same time it called for rigid maintenance of price ceilings and control of expenditures through measures of rationing, taxation, and savings. In the following year, the union again asked for similar concessions and in addition demanded a company-financed sick-leave pay plan.

These attempts to broaden the scope of collective bargaining through the War Labor Board were unsuccessful. The Board denied the union's requests for such measures as employment guarantees, industry-wide wage stabilization, and sick-leave pay on the grounds that it did not have authority to consider such measures. The Board, it was obvious, was not willing to set new patterns of fundamental union-management relations which might be carried over into peacetime operation.

As the war came to a close in 1945 and war contracts were cancelled, the Reuther group presented still another program for national production planning: that government-owned war plants be converted to the mass production of railroad equipment and low-cost housing. The plan recommended that Congress set up two public authorities similar in organization and function to the TVA: a Housing Production Authority and a Railroad Equipment Authority. This plan for the creation of government-owned yardstick plants in the traditional fields of private enterprise indicated that the union was prepared to press its ideas of economic planning in a peacetime economy. The program stressed that the "people's investment" (over twenty billion dollars in production facilities purchased with war bond receipts) was largely concentrated in government-owned facilities in heavy and basic industries and should be employed in the people's interest. The Authorities could "(1) lease plants to private manufacturers to be operated as part of the program; (2) directly operate government-owned plants; (3) lease plants to workers' producer cooperatives to be operated as part of the program." The plan cited plants adaptable to mass production of housing and indicated a great need of low-cost prefabricated housing. It went into considerable detail concerning the minimum requirements which such a program should meet, such as establishing equitable wage patterns, providing a low priced product, protecting government investment. It outlined the kinds of plants and the numbers of workers which would be idled by cessation of the war.[7]

This plan, which was not supported by the left-wing faction of the UAW, never got far because the anticipated volume of reconversion unemployment did not materialize. Instead, the problem of postwar inflation was uppermost in the minds of workers. The union's next attack was centered on this problem.

In the fall of 1945 the UAW brought the program of planning squarely into the arena of collective bargaining. In negotiations with General Motors the UAW asked for wage increases without price increases.[8] The union maintained that prices, profits, and production levels were

---

[7] Walter P. Reuther, *Are War Plants Expendable?* (Ypsilanti, Michigan: Local 50, UAW-CIO, July 1945).

[8] *Purchasing Power for Prosperity* (Detroit: GM Department, UAW-CIO, November, 1945). A brief presented to General Motors by the UAW-CIO in support of its demands for 30 per cent hourly wage increases with no increase in automobile prices.

matters which should be considered in wage negotiations with a corporation like General Motors which might set a pattern for the rest of industry. In following this course of action the union was bidding for the support not just of auto workers and labor, but of the public as well. The union statements stressed that the UAW wanted "to make progress with the community, not at the expense of the community." The corporation, however, refused to include cost, profit, and price issues in the negotiations. Although the long strike over this issue failed to budge the corporation from its position, the "consumer-oriented" wage policy expounded in the November 1945 brief persisted in subsequent statements of the UAW[9] and the CIO.[10]

The wage-price policy of UAW-CIO in 1945 was the most determined attempt by the Reuther forces to establish the principle that the economic problems of auto workers could be solved only by some sort of overall planning in the basic industries and in the national economy. The immediate objective was to take the lead in increasing wage rates to compensate for decreases in take-home pay, while keeping the lid on prices. The significant point is that the union stated that it was as deeply concerned with prices and means of holding them down as with increases in money wages. In this connection, the program was much more than an ordinary demand for wage in-

---

[9] Walter Reuther, *Members, Workers, Consumers, Citizens* (Detroit: UAW-CIO, April, 1946). *UAW-CIO Wage Policy Statement* (Detroit: UAW-CIO, October, 1946). *Statement of UAW-CIO Executive Board* (Detroit: UAW-CIO, Dec. 18, 1946). *United Automobile Worker*, January, 1947. Walter Reuther, speech before UAW-CIO Foundry Conference at Milwaukee, Wis., Dec. 7, 1946.

[10] Robert N. Nathan Associates, *A National Wage Policy for 1947* (Washington: Robert N. Nathan Associates, 1947). An economic analysis prepared for the CIO. Philip Murray, statements to the press, December, 1946, and January, 1947.

creases; it was an attempt to marshal political and economic forces in support of government and industry price control and to make price policies a factor in collective bargaining. Despite the fact that the opposing faction in the UAW, as well as other large CIO unions, did not support the specific Reuther strategy in its strike against General Motors over the wage-price issues, the Reuther followers have continued to support the contention that planning is necessary in order to avoid an inflationary spiral and a deflationary bust. The various programs which they advanced during and immediately after the war were, in effect, manifestations of a philosophy basic to this group.

The Aims and Goals of the Reuther Forces

The Reuther programs during these years were aimed at finding some solution to the problem of economic insecurity. The policies and programs of his group had strong appeal not only to auto workers but to many other classes of industrial workers in whose minds economic security was practically synonymous with freedom. The group's objectives were freedom from want, freedom from unemployment, and freedom from fear of insecurity. Reuther believed the achievement of these objectives involved conscious planning. The UAW group did not believe that security could be assured by the interplay of blind economic forces in a planless society.

The persistent thread of a program for "transforming a formless anarchic economy into a rational industrial society"[11] ran through all of the Reuther proposals. In one phase, national economic planning (broad social insurance, government housing programs, a peace production

---

[11] See in particular Victor G. Reuther's article, "The Next Fifty Years," *Detroit,* June, 1945.

board, etc.) was proposed. Appeals were made to the public and to the government for action. At other times, collective bargaining became the center of attention as when the union proposed industry-wide wage stabilization, the annual wage, and jointly administered company or industry sickness and old age insurance plans.

The union also carried on a continuous drive to link the workers' fight for security with a broader quest for security by other sympathetic non-labor groups. Wherever possible the community interest was tied to the union's goals, such as it was in the announced policy of "no wage increases at the expense of the community."

Reuther stated quite clearly his belief that privately owned business which exploited its privilege of freedom in the interests of stockholders would lead inevitably to the shattering of the common man's faith in free enterprise. General Motors was pictured as an irresponsible industrial octopus which opposed with its political and economic power the efforts of the common man to achieve freedom through guaranteed security. Reuther's purpose was to make both workers and the public distrustful of unregulated and uncontrolled "big business."

Reuther did not state, however, that he was for socialization of industry or for elimination of the system of private enterprise. He did indicate that an economy which failed to guarantee freedom from unemployment and insecurity also failed to meet the expectations and desires of the American people. To the extent that people were considered more important than enterprise and the public interest was put ahead of profits, Reuther had no quarrel with the private enterprise system. He was convinced, however, that free enterprise had so far failed to insure a secure economy. He was advocating a "planned" private enterprise system as a means of making production responsive to the needs of a dynamic society. In his article "The Challenge of Peace," Reuther wrote:

> I have nothing against free enterprise. But American working men and women are interested in realities, not slogans; in jobs, not rosy promises.
>
> Free enterprise can only be justified if it brings freedom from want, freedom from unemployment, and freedom from fear of insecurity.
>
> My conception of free enterprise does not mean license for private institutions to exploit a privilege; it does mean the obligation of an institution, no matter who owns it, to so conduct itself as to serve the public interest.[12]

Some labor leaders and some labor historians might argue that the Reuther group would outgrow its notions of planning and its leaders would end up as "pure and simple" trade unionists when the group reached matur-

---

[12] A full version of Reuther's statement on the limits of free enterprise follows:

"I have nothing against free enterprise. But American working men and women are interested in realities, not slogans; in jobs, not rosy promises. Free enterprise today is more a slogan than a reality. Business can make promises but, without the cooperation of labor and government, it cannot deliver the jobs and the goods. We did not have free enterprise before the war: monopolies in many industries had long been restricting production, and government was obliged to play an increasing role in all the economic processes. Yet even so six to ten million American citizens were unemployed.

"The hard fact is that almost the only time in our history when we have had steady full employment and maximum production has been in this war. I do not see how we can hope to achieve those goals after the war unless we keep up a high level of effective demand such as we now have. Free enterprise can only be justified if it brings freedom from want, freedom from unemployment, and freedom from fear of insecurity.

"Free enterprise can have a definite place in our postwar plans. But when I use the term 'free enterprise' I do not use it with the same meaning it has for the National Association of Manufacturers. Enterprise does not have to be privately owned to be free. It *may* be privately owned and remain free. It may be publicly owned, as the TVA is publicly owned, and remain free. It may be co-operatively owned, as the Rochdale co-operatives are owned, and remain free. This is not the meaning that the NAM gives

ity. Other observers have already pointed out that Reuther had been striving for broad social and political leadership, and that sooner or later these goals and ambitions would prove to be inconsistent with advancing the particular interests of automobile workers as a narrow producers' group. Still others maintained that Reuther had talked too much and should have kept his mouth shut. The attacks made upon Reuther by the opposing faction in the UAW-CIO were bitter and vehement. In a pamphlet issued as UAW election campaign literature in 1946, Reuther was described as a "Young-Man-In-A-Hurry" who led the workers astray in the General Motors strike of 1945–46. The idea that "prices can be set by collective bargaining" was called "phony," and the impression was created that Reuther's idea as expressed in magazine articles and news releases, while serving his

---

to the term 'free enterprise.' NAM believes in the privilege of privately-owned enterprise to govern itself according to its own interests, regardless of what the public and social consequences may be.

"When a corporation does as it pleases, no matter what happens to the public welfare, it is not enjoying freedom; on the contrary, it is exploiting a privilege. My conception of free enterprise does not mean license for private institutions to exploit a privilege; it does mean the obligation of an institution, no matter who owns it, to so conduct itself as to serve the public interest.

"There is a definite place in our postwar planning for privately-owned free enterprise which does a good job for the public. We should encourage firms which compete with entrenched monopolies and offer the public a better product at a lower price. We should encourage all small businesses which challenge those enterprises that restrict production and fix prices. We should provide ample credit resources for new enterprises designed to fill a public need—even if they do compete with old and inefficient businesses. So long as a privately-owned enterprise is efficient; so long as it competes in a free market to offer the consumer a desirable product; so long as it reinvests its profits, expands its plants and passes the benefits of technological progress on to the consumer and labor; and so long as it permits its employees to organize freely and bargain collectively to protect their rights and interests—that enterprise is serving the public. Such enterprises do not need to be rigidly supervised by government. They do a good job and deserve credit for it." "The Challenge of Peace," *International Post War Problems,* II (April 1945), 6–7.

personal political fortunes, also resulted in prolonging the strike unnecessarily. Reuther, indeed, has continued to have many enemies both within and without the labor movement.

It has always been clear that Reuther's major decisions associated with implementation of his long-range objectives have had to be made in the light of his political position. As his opponents within the union directly or indirectly opposed many of his specific plans (such as the 1945–46 GM strike strategy and his program for postwar conversion of war plants to government production authorities), the timing and tactical detail of every union program has had to take into consideration not only the national political and economic picture, and the current aspirations of and pressure from auto workers, but also the political orientation of factional opponents as well. Yet the significant feature about Reuther's factional fights has been that they have appeared to influence timing and detail of individual strategies but have not required deviations from the essence of the Reuther philosophy. The union group which has faced General Motors has had firm convictions and a clear-cut philosophy. It has pursued them persistently and openly. For this reason, the Reuther group has been continually under attack both from within the labor movement and from the companies under contract with the UAW.

Decision-Making in the UAW

To match better the bargaining power of General Motors, the UAW found it expedient to consolidate and exert the strength of its separate GM locals through a central GM Department. Reuther became director of this department at its inception, and under his leadership it has spearheaded the drive to expand the scope of collective bargaining with GM, and at the same time it has handled the day-to-day problems of labor relations with the corporation.

While Reuther has been known for his nationally publicized plans, the GM Department has also been known for its painstaking job of coordinating local union demands and administering the GM contract. The decision-making processes involved in getting the union's labor relations work done has been more complex and unpredictable than corresponding decisions on the management side. As head of a union characterized by factional struggles and a militant spirit among its rank and file, Reuther has faced the difficult task of centralizing and integrating its policy and administration.

For many years decisions on major union policy and contract terms have been worked out in meetings of the GM councils and the GM Department staff. The formal organization of this group has been as follows: In regional GM sub-councils each GM local union is represented by its president, chairman of the shop committee, and one delegate for each 5,000 workers in the plant. Each of these sub-councils elects a chairman who serves on the national GM negotiating committee. The sub-councils meet to discuss mutual problems and to pass resolutions and demands for transmission to higher authority.

The National GM Council is composed of representatives from the nine sub-councils (about 250 delegates). This group meets regularly three times a year. It meets more frequently during periods of crisis. The GM sub-councils' demands are discussed with the GM Department staff at these meetings and the council makes decisions on policy and strategy for negotiations. The GM Council and the sub-councils make up the specific legislative branch of the UAW-GM setup. The UAW-GM Department serves as the administrative arm.

The essentials of an over-all strategy have always been formulated by Reuther and a group of economic and political experts in the International Union headquarters. These experts have been sprinkled among the education, publicity, and consumer departments of the union as well as on Reuther's personal staff. To date, they have been largely Reuther's appointees selected on the basis of specific abilities and sympathy with Reuther's fundamental union philosophy.

At the GM Council meetings, specific demands of the delegates have been woven into the framework of each major program. The Council delegates have had the authority to instruct Reuther and his staff to implement or to discontinue programs and policies and to accept or decline contract terms. However, by developing programs which had strong appeal to the membership, Reuther has been usually successful in winning the support of the local leadership.

The GM Department has always been subject to the control of the executive board of the International Union. Although a great deal of autonomy has been allowed, the various activities of this department which bear directly on the union as a whole must be discussed and authorized by the International executive board. The greatest factional battles have occurred at this point.[13]

The UAW-GM Department staff has acted as interpreter, coordinator and administrator of the national UAW-GM contract and as court lawyer in processing

---

[13] The executive board has consisted of the president, two vice-presidents, financial secretary, and twenty-two regional directors, all elected at annual conventions. The "top officers" were elected by all delegates and the regional directors by delegates from their respective regions. In 1947 the majority of the board were members of the caucus opposing Reuther.

grievances to the umpire. The staff has maintained a united front in negotiations with General Motors. Centralized contract administration came to be recognized among the membership as essential in day-to-day dealing with the corporation.

The relationship between the GM Department and the local unions has not been one of superior to inferior as in the normal management hierarchy. Rather, it has been a relationship of reciprocal responsibility, in which the local unions have demanded such services from the GM Department as assistance in local negotiations and the processing of unadjusted grievances to the umpire. The GM Department in turn has demanded cooperation and contract discipline from the local unions. The control exercised by the UAW-GM staff in this regard was reflected in the war strike record. Staff representatives repeatedly "straightened out" threatened wildcat strike situations and in some cases held restless membership in check for a matter of years awaiting War Labor Board decisions on their disputes with the General Motors Corporation.[14]

Conclusion

The Reuther supporters, largely in control of the local unions throughout the General Motors Corporation, have had a clear-cut notion of the functions and limitations of traditional collective bargaining as well as a blueprint for future collective bargaining and broad economic planning. The Reuther group has been more determined in pressing for its long-range goals than most unions in the country because of its deep convictions and strong beliefs in these goals. It has sought support for its program

---

[14] In this connection, however, the success of the union in maintaining order was in part due to the determination of the corporation to discipline workers taking part in stoppages. See page 47.

from non-labor as well as labor groups in the community; it has placed strong reliance on political action as a partner to collective bargaining. Reuther has been seeking the leadership of a social group of which the working classes are only a part.

In a union in which factionalism has been a chronic problem, Reuther has lined up most of the union officers in GM plants behind his programs. The careful timing and appeal of his economic plans, his political maneuvers, and his services to local unions, apparently unified his support. For these reasons, in times of crisis insurgencies among GM locals have been relatively minor. Under pressure, the GM locals could be counted on for well-disciplined action. The union which has faced General Motors has been a strong, militant organization. The corporation, equally strong and determined, has stood in its path.

THE CORPORATION FACES THE UNION

General Motors, like the UAW-CIO, has had concrete ideas about the function of collective bargaining. Furthermore, it has developed a philosophy concerning broader social goals which is more clear cut than that of most corporations. It has an economic plan just as the union has. Our purpose here is to analyze the structure of beliefs, attitudes and reactions which are important for an understanding of the part the corporation has been playing in labor-management relations.

The Collective Bargaining Policy of General Motors

During the first decade of union-management relations General Motors developed a labor relations policy that was administered with consistency and rigidity throughout its organization. This policy evolved out of experience in meeting union pressures, particularly those applied by the UAW. Other large corporations have developed definite labor relations policies, but few have been as successful as General Motors in getting them accepted and enforced by their organizations. Outside observers seem to be agreed that General Motors has always known what its objectives were in bargaining with unions. Even Walter Reuther has remarked, "General Motors is tough, but it does have policies."

The authors found that the main elements of the labor relations policy as applied throughout General Motors have been as follows:

First, "labor relations" have meant relations with the unions which are the legal representatives of employees for purposes of collective bargaining. A distinction has been made between "employee relations" and "labor relations." General Motors never surrendered its right to have direct contact with its employees on matters not coming within the scope of collective bargaining as defined by law or union contracts. Management at all levels has spoken of "bargaining with unions" and "dealings with our employees" as separate and distinct functions.

Second, contrary to beliefs widely held, General Motors apparently has not been trying to break the unions representing the hourly rated employees. The corporation's executives have seemed to feel that even if they could get rid of the existing unions, new labor organizations would sooner or later spring up which might be more difficult to deal with than those already in existence. The nub of the General Motors labor relations policy has been to contain unions, and to restrict relations with them.

Third, as a means of containing unions, General Motors has striven constantly to confine collective bargaining in particular and management-union relations in general to the narrow issues of wages, hours, and conditions of employment. General Motors has specified those matters it regards as falling in the area of management's responsibility and those which are subject to joint determination.

For example, in its agreement with the UAW, as in its agreements with other unions, the corporation has reserved the right to hire, promote, and discharge for cause. It has retained sole responsibility for the maintenance of discipline and efficiency of employees. It likewise has retained unrestricted authority to determine the products to be manufactured, the location of plants, the schedules of production, and the methods, processes, and means of manufacturing. The corporation has also kept the specific right to discipline any employee for taking part in any violation of the no-strike section of the agreement. The subjects for negotiation within the scope of collective bargaining include rates of pay, wages, hours of work, seniority rules and regulations as they apply to lay-offs and rehiring, methods and procedures for adjudication of grievances, and other related conditions of employment. The union has been free to challenge the disciplinary actions of management in individual cases. If no satisfactory settlements were reached, such matters were adjudicated by the permanent, impartial umpire (employed jointly by the UAW and General Motors) to whom the corporation had by agreement delegated the power to review its disciplinary action.

Fourth, General Motors has made a practice of exercising its managerial rights up and down the line. With very few exceptions, employees deemed responsible for stoppages, slowdowns or other violations of the agreement have been disciplined by the corporation. From the outset the corporation has been willing to have entire plants shut down completely rather than back water on disciplinary action taken against a handful of union members. The umpire has consistently sustained the position of the corporation where such disciplinary action has been taken for just cause. Consequently, the corporation has striven to discipline anyone responsible for a major violation of the agreement or for any concerted interference with production schedules and working force efficiency. In such matters the policy of General Motors has been to be very tough.

Fifth, General Motors has opposed joint union-management responsibilities of all kinds. The corporation has not allowed the union to participate with management in making decisions involving disciplinary actions, production standards, wage payment systems, or any other matters whether they fall outside or within its definition of the scope of collective bargaining. The guiding principle has been that management made decisions and initiated action which the union may challenge. The corporation seldom has discussed its proposed actions in advance with the union. When it has sounded out the union on measures it proposed to take, it made sure that the "discussions" did not result in "negotiations" of any kind.

For example, during the war General Motors refused to go along with the government-sponsored plan for establishment of plant union-management "production committees." Such joint committees did operate in a few of its plants, but their actions were restricted to slogan campaigns and other trivial matters—even these were frowned on by the top officials of the corporation. Many executives have expressed pride in not falling for "that joint-committee ballyhoo" sponsored by the government during the war. This same opposition to joint responsibilities has extended even to safety committees, recreational programs, social activities, and community fund drives.

Sixth, General Motors has been opposed not only to delegating managerial functions to unions, but also to any other "outsiders." In the agreements with the UAW, for example, the powers of the permanent umpire have been rigidly and specifically prescribed. Grievances relating to production standards or the establishment or change of any wage rate have not been subject to review by the umpire. In the event of failure to dispose of such grievances in accordance with the established procedure, the parties have been free to resort to the strike or lockout. Management would rather stand a strike over these issues which it has felt were vital than jeopardize them in a case before an arbitrator or umpire.

The corporation also has resisted persistently advice or pressures from government officials and even employer associations. During the war many of the automobile companies submitted to the pressures of Army or Navy procurement officers. To insure continued production of war materiel, these officers often made suggestions regarding company labor policies. Sometimes they assisted companies in exercising discipline, and occasionally they intervened directly in a strike or stoppage. General Motors, however, continued to run its plants according to the contract, and it permitted no intervention by outside parties which was not provided for in the contract.[15]

Seventh, the General Motors top executives have seemed convinced that the establishment of and adherence to its policy have been more important than the settlement of specific issues and specific problems which arose in the course of collective bargaining. The corporation has striven to avoid compromise on policies and resort to expediency, even if such a course of action involved expenditure of resources. General Motors executives in-

---

[15] Actually, these officers did not have clear-cut authority to inject themselves into labor relations matters, but where continued production was threatened, they could make patriotic appeals or threaten to recommend withdrawal of war contracts. General Motors claimed that these "outsiders" often wanted companies to forego disciplinary action in the interest of temporary expediency.

tend to keep themselves in the managerial driver's seat. They seem prepared to fight to establish and to preserve that status and the principles which it represents.

To sum it all up, the authors found that General Motors has striven to be "tough but fair" in the administration of labor relations. It has insisted upon rigid adherence to the letter of union contracts by all levels of management as well as by the union. Most General Motors executives have thought that the "be tough and fair" policy paid off. They have indicated that this tough policy made the union respect the contract, and gave the union the power to keep its members in line in the plants. Management has felt that because of this policy it has been exercising discipline and maintaining authority in its plants while in some other corporations the unions have been dangerously close to "taking over." This approach has been more than a method of dealing with unions; it has been also a means of maintaining the self-respect and the morale of management as a group.

The rationale of this labor relations policy can be better appreciated if we examine the feelings and attitudes of General Motors executives towards unions in general and the UAW-CIO in particular. On several occasions, C. E. Wilson, president of the corporation, has indicated that the UAW has had three guiding principles: first, to get more pay for less work; second, to free workers from the discipline and authority of management; third, to conduct a hate campaign designed to undermine the loyalty of workers to the corporation. This summarizes General Motors' reasons for resentment toward the UAW.

Another complaint has been that the UAW officials (and for that matter, the officials of other unions with which the corporation dealt) have been motivated in collective bargaining by political expediency rather than sound reasoning. To substantiate this belief, General Motors executives have pointed to the factional cleavages within the UAW and have cited many instances of where the "union bureaucrats" have resorted to political maneuvers to maintain themselves in power.

It is important to note, however, that General Motors executives have repeatedly stated both publicly and privately that they believe in collective bargaining. They have been firmly convinced that it has a proper place in modern industrial society. But in their opinion, collective bargaining should never be allowed to interfere with the exercise of management's authority and functions. This emphasis upon a rigid line between union responsibility and management functions has resulted in a policy of deliberately keeping the relationship between union and management officials on an "arm's length" basis. In broader terms, collective bargaining has been looked upon as a bulkhead whose function has been to provide, as Alfred P. Sloan stated, "an irresistible force against encroachments on the competitive system of enterprise on the part of any outside influence."[16]

Obviously, General Motors' concept of "collective bargaining" has been diametrically opposed to that of the UAW. The parties have used the same term to express widely differing concepts and beliefs.

The Philosophy of Management

Because of General Motors' size and dominant position in the automotive industry, its critics often have referred to the corporation as a vast aggregate of monopoly power. In the opinion of its executives, however, General Motors has been an efficient and highly competitive enterprise which has developed an organizational structure

---

[16] Alfred P. Sloan, Jr., *Why the Confusion* (Detroit: General Motors Corporation, Nov. 13, 1946).

that effectively answers the problems of modern industrial society.

Over the years the guiding organizational principle at General Motors has come to be "decentralized operations and responsibilities with coordinated control." Alfred P. Sloan, chairman of the board of General Motors, and his associates developed the concept of decentralization into a philosophy of management and a system of local self-government in industry.[17]

Under this principle of organization, central management has set the broad goals and policies of the corporation, limited and defined the authority of the divisional managers, relieved divisional management of responsibility for problems not strictly connected with production and sales, and offered its services and help to divisions in a staff capacity. From this point on the divisional managers have had responsibility for the production and sale of the products they manufacture. Peter Drucker has described this organizational setup as an "essay in federalism" com-

---

[17] A good analysis of the philosophy and management structure is developed by Peter F. Drucker in his recent book entitled *Concept of the Corporation*. On page 46, for example, Drucker summarizes the concept of decentralization as follows:

"Decentralization, as the term is usually understood, means division of labor and is nothing new. In fact, it is one of the prerequisites of any management, whether that of a business or of an army. But in General Motors usage, decentralization is much more than that. In over twenty years of work, first from 1923 to 1937 as President, since then as Chairman of the Corporation, Mr. Alfred P. Sloan, Jr., has developed the concept of decentralization into a philosophy of industrial management and into a system of local self-government. It is not a mere technique of management but an outline of a social order. Decentralization in General Motors is not confined to the relations between divisional managers and central management but is to extend in theory to all managerial positions including that of foreman; it is not confined in its operation within the company but extends to the relations to its partners in business, particularly the automobile dealers; and for Mr. Sloan and his associates the application and further extension of decentralization are the answer to most of the problems of modern industrial society." *Concept of the Corporation* (New York: The John Day Company, 1946).

bining the greatest corporate unity with the greatest divisional autonomy and responsibility. Like a federation, General Motors has attempted to achieve unity of broad goals through a sort of local self-government.

In many respects the divisions have always made up a kind of competitive system within the corporation. The Oldsmobile Division, for example, is said to compete with the Pontiac Division in the sale of automobiles in the same price range. Likewise, many of the parts manufacturing divisions may compete among themselves and with independent vendors in selling parts to GM's car and truck manufacturing divisions. General Motors officials have said repeatedly that this kind of competition is necessary to stimulate initiative in the individual and to promote efficient management of business enterprise. They have held that in a large corporation there must be internal as well as external competition to provide the proper incentives for company executives. A top official of General Motors expressed this idea in these words:

> General Motors could accurately be termed as a free enterprise system within the free enterprise system. The formulation of corporation policy within the framework of which freedom of action can be exercised corresponds to the body of law within the framework of which all industrial enterprise is carried on. . . . . It is particularly significant, in the instance of General Motors, that arbitrary power of central authority has never been exercised, even though ability to do so and a full sense of over-all responsibility have existed at all times. . . .[18]

GM officials have resented bitterly any insinuations that they have used dictatorial management methods, fixed prices or restricted trade in the fields in which they operate. They firmly believe that General Motors, as presently organized, is a good working example of efficient and competitive free enterprise at its best. Being thus

---

[18] Donaldson Brown (vice-chairman of General Motors Corporation), *Industrial Management as a National Resource* (Detroit: General Motors Corporation, March 18, 1943).

convinced of the virtues of the General Motors system, the corporation's executives have been prepared to stave off interference from two sources—from unions and from the government. Like the UAW, they have been anxious to identify their particular philosophy and program (which have been diametrically opposed to those of the union) with the broader interests of society.

Goals and Objectives

General Motors, accordingly, has had a plan and a program just as the UAW has had a plan and a program. It has argued that the common good is best served by doing those things that reduce real costs and increase productive efficiency. In the words of C. E. Wilson, president of General Motors, "Increases in productivity are not automatic, nor are they, generally speaking, the result of increased effort by workers. They result from improved tools, new processes and new inventions, and these come about because someone is willing to put up money for their development—in the hope of making a profit."[19]

General Motors executives have maintained that increased productivity depends upon maintaining freedom for private enterprise. It cannot be achieved by any kind of joint economic planning or by a "something-for-nothing" philosophy. On this basis, the corporation has consistently attacked the "New Deal philosophy" and most New Deal programs (both of which, of course, lay very close to the hearts of the UAW leadership). For example, C. E. Wilson has criticized the whole philosophy of the New Deal's social security program. In a talk at Mount Union College in Alliance, Ohio, on October 18, 1946, he made this statement:

---

[19] C. E. Wilson, speech to United States Conference of Mayors, Washington, D.C., Jan. 21, 1947 (Detroit: General Motors Corporation, 1947), p. 14.

> Security is like happiness, as many individuals have found. If you put it first and make it your aim, you lose it. Security is like peace, as many a country has found. If you make it an isolated object of policy, you lose it.
>
> I think this is the truth which is at the back of the minds of those who fear that schemes of social security may sap people's initiative and enterprise and rob them of the will to work. They see the need of a spirit of effort, initiative and adventure, and I agree with them. . . .
>
> I agree that if people have security and no purpose, no sense of loyalty to something beyond themselves, they will lapse into their shell. I agree that these are dangers in security alone.

"Economic statesmanship," as viewed by top management of General Motors, has been "first and above all a recognition of the prime importance of technology," which has been "the motivating center of all real progress." The quest for progress must apply to all functional aspects of enterprise including distribution, labor relations, and organization and management techniques. But all these things must be directed to "creation of new and useful things" and to "selling existing products at lower prices."[20]

To the extent that a management promotes progress, it has, in the view of the corporation, promoted the common good on the basis that what has been good for the corporation has been in the best interest of the nation. To the extent that industry discharges this responsibility, the only type of "planning" needed is that done by the millions of customers who in effect are the only real bosses of the economy.

In a speech in the fall of 1944, Alfred P. Sloan declared that the "something-for-nothing" philosophy which prevailed in the thirties was dead and that the election of Governor Dewey as President of the United States would bring about some of the changes needed to bolster the private enterprise system. "It took something like fourteen

---

[20] Alfred P. Sloan, Jr., *The Importance of Jobs* (Detroit: General Motors Corporation, Nov. 15, 1944), pp. 11–12.

years to rid this country of prohibition," he explained. "It is going to take a good while to rid the country of the New Deal economic philosophy. These things take time, but sooner or later the axe falls and we get a change."[21] In 1946, Sloan attacked unions as labor monopolies and proposed governmental curbs on their power. He advocated the application of the principles of the Sherman Act to unions as a fair and equitable means of requiring both business and labor to conform to the fundamental principles of a competitive economy.[22]

The viewpoint of the corporation, particularly as it has pertained to unions and to collective bargaining, has been set forth in greater detail by its president, C. E. Wilson. In his statement before the Senate Committee on Labor and Public Welfare in February, 1947, Wilson made specific recommendations not only for the regulation of unions but for the restriction by law of the scope of collective bargaining as well.[23] "The monopoly power of national and international unions," he said, "must be curbed by law." He advocated especially prohibition of industry-wide bargaining which, if carried to its logical conclusion, he claimed, would destroy our free competitive system. He proposed that compulsory union membership should be outlawed and declared in response to questioning that he would "return to the farm" before signing a closed shop agreement with unions. Like many other industrialists, he also advocated the outlawing of secondary boycotts, sympathy strikes and jurisdictional strikes, exclusion of foremen from provisions of the Na-

---

[21] Alfred P. Sloan, Jr., speech before the Chamber of Commerce of the State of New York as reported in *The New York Times,* Oct. 6, 1944.

[22] Alfred P. Sloan, Jr., speech before the Boston Chamber of Commerce as reported in the *Chicago Sun,* Dec. 20, 1946.

[23] C. E. Wilson, *Legislation for Labor Peace.* A statement made before the United States Senate Committee on Labor and Public Welfare, Feb. 5, 1947 (Detroit: General Motors Corporation, 1947).

tional Labor Relations Act, revision of the Act in order to "equalize" the position of management and labor and the prohibition of other abuses by organized labor.

Wilson's proposal to limit the scope of collective bargaining was perhaps most important and significant. He charged that the National Labor Relations Act of 1935 left the way open for ambitious union leaders to revolutionize our form of society. In the course of his remarks, he made this striking statement:

> Only by defining and restricting collective bargaining to its proper sphere can we hope to save what we have come to know as our American system and keep it from evolving into an alien form, imported from east of the Rhine. Unless this is done, *the border area of collective bargaining will be a constant battleground between employers and unions, as the unions continuously attempt to press the boundary farther and farther into the area of managerial functions.*[24]

The relation of the corporation's objectives in political action to its policy of containing unions in the process of collective bargaining is easy to understand. Although General Motors has been successful in retaining its managerial functions at its own plants, it has sought continuously to fortify its position and that of other employers by advocating amendment of the Wagner Act to specify that "only rates of pay, hours of employment and the circumstances and conditions under which employees actually perform work, come within the area of collective bargaining required by the Act." In his testimony in 1947, Wilson was specific in his opposition to inclusion of pension, health and welfare plans within the permissible area of collective bargaining. Although he indicated that employees should be free to participate in employer-sponsored or union-sponsored plans of this nature, he claimed that any attempt to develop them jointly through collective bargaining would create "new and unexplored

---

[24] *Ibid.*, p. 14. Italics inserted.

areas of industrial disputes, difficult—if not impossible—to solve."

In summary, the aim of General Motors on the legislative front has been to have laws enacted which would curb the power of labor organizations and confine the relationships between unions and employers to bargaining over wages, hours and conditions of employment on an individual company basis. This has been consistent with the corporation's policy of limiting the activities of unions in its own plants. This has been consistent also with its basic desire to preserve private enterprise and management's position of leadership in the economy. General Motors has had a carefully thought out and consistent approach to the "union problem." It has known where it wanted to go.

The Process of Decision-Making in Labor Relations

The decision-making power on labor relation policy as on other matters has centered around the chairman of the board, the president, and three executive vice-presidents. These five officials have formed a team. They have worked closely with three committees—the financial policy committee, the operations policy committee, and the administration committee. On these committees, in addition to these men, have been the senior staff and administrative officers of the corporation as well as representatives of the major stockholding interests. These committees, together with the board of directors, have constituted what might be called the top government of General Motors, and have made all major decisions on policy.

The policy planning on labor relations has been done by a specialized group called the personnel policy committee, headed by the vice-president in charge of personnel and composed of senior line executives of the corporation, division managers, and labor relations staff specialists. The deliberations of this group have been passed up to the administration committee for approval.

The decision-making process in General Motors has been neither formal nor mechanical. Decisions have been reached as a result of group deliberation. Individuals particularly affected by the policy under discussion have been given an opportunity to talk things out. In contrast to the UAW, there have been no clearly defined factions in General Motors' top management. There have been, of course, sharply different points of view among various executives on specific issues. These different points of view, and the alignment of certain groups with similar points of view, have sometimes shifted with the issues under discussion. In spite of its size, however, General Motors has been able to determine policies effectively and get them followed down the line. Once a decision was made, all General Motors executives have gone along with it and no one has attempted to take issue with it.

Within the broad framework of established policy the labor relations staff of the vice-president in charge of personnel has controlled the administration of labor relations throughout the corporation. Specifically, this labor relations staff has performed these functions: (1) contract negotiation and renegotiation, (2) supervision of contract administration, (3) preparation and handling of appeal cases to the corporation and the umpire, and (4) hourly wage administration.

The day-to-day handling of labor relations has been a responsibility assumed at the division and plant levels. In each division there has been a personnel or industrial relations director with a staff reporting to the divisional manager. In addition to other duties in the area of personnel administration, the divisional personnel director has been responsible for seeing that the divisional management at all levels has kept in line with the labor relations policies of the corporation. The divisional managers and factory superintendents usually have gone to the divisional personnel director for guidance on labor relations policy. The personnel director in turn has received his instructions concerning such policies from the corporation's labor relations staff in Detroit.

The central controls over administration of labor relations can be illustrated by a few examples. The corporation-wide agreement with the UAW has made provision for local supplementary agreements on such issues as the application of seniority, wage scales, wage payment plans, new job rates and shift preference. All such supplementary agreements have had to be approved by the Detroit labor relations staff (as well as by the GM Department of the UAW-CIO). The staff has carefully scrutinized them for possible conflict with the general agreement and for the effect they might have on operating policies in other plants and divisions. The approval of local wage agreements, furthermore, has extended even to establishment of individual wage rates on new jobs.

Of necessity, the final steps in the grievance procedure were centralized because most unsettled grievances were subject to review by the umpire. Since the Detroit labor relations staff has controlled all appeals to the umpire, the divisional personnel managers usually discussed critical grievances with members of this staff long before they reached the appeal stage. The divisions have disliked being reversed by higher authority on cases of this kind; hence, they have been prone to consult Detroit before making what often appeared to be rather petty decisions.

Finally, the general agreement applying to all plants where the UAW was recognized has been in itself an instrument of central control. This agreement, spelled out in eighty-six printed pages in 1946, has been the "labor relations legislation" of the corporation and has provided the basis for the decisions of the umpire, who gradually has developed a body of precedents built up by decisions in hundreds of cases. All management personnel throughout General Motors have been required to conform to the letter of "the little grey book" and its interpretations in the form of umpire rulings.

Why should labor relations be so highly centralized in a far-flung organization which has operated in other phases of business management on a decentralized basis? In the first place, the relationship between the corporation and the UAW has been very much like that of an armed truce. On fundamental issues, the parties have had conflicting interests and viewpoints. Each has been extremely suspicious of the motives and actions of the other. Through experience the corporation learned that the union would use concessions secured in one plant as a means of pressing its demands in others. Central control has existed as a guard against the "inchworm tactics" of the union. The entire strategy of "containing the union" could be wrecked by union encroachments at the weak points in management's organization.

In the second place, the development of a strategy for dealing with a union, which has been constantly striving to use General Motors as a pattern-setter in labor relations, has called for a high order of intelligence and training among management personnel. The implications of the factional cleavages and internal policies of the UAW-CIO have been fully understood only by the most sophisticated of labor relations experts. These experts, like members of the intelligence staff of an army, have had to be in a position to anticipate the tactics of the other side. Decisions which might ultimately affect the whole corporation could not be left to the judgment of hundreds of divisional managers and personnel directors. Those down the line might not be well informed on the details of what was transpiring throughout the corporation and in some cases might not have mastered the fine points of even ordinary management-union strategy. It has been logical, under such conditions, that the area of local managerial discretion in labor relations matters should be narrowly circumscribed. The very size of the corporation and the fact that it has been a major target of UAW pressure has made such a policy plausible in the light of the issues involved.

Conclusion

The policies and objectives of General Motors, though entirely different from those of the UAW, have involved definite and clear-cut principles concerning the appropriate function of collective bargaining as well as the necessary area of political action.

Undoubtedly, those responsible for policy determination in General Motors have felt that the corporation's labor relations program has made for more efficient operations. Its strike record under contracts, for example, was thought to be far superior to that of most other automobile companies. There is no way of isolating in dollars and cents the contribution of this labor relations program to the profit and loss statement. But as one executive expressed it, "General Motors has been profitable because of good management, and our labor relations policy is just one phase of that good management."

It would appear also that executives get just as much satisfaction out of running a business efficiently (and getting credit for so running it) as they do from making money for the stockholders. Such satisfactions are great, indeed, in running an industrial system the size of General Motors. Within General Motors, as within comparable corporations, there has been a management group distinct both from the ownership group (the stockholders) and the worker group. The management group has been in between the workers and the stockholders. This group has been interested in preserving its authority and status as professional management. Since it has had responsibility for the direction and operation of the business, it naturally has wanted to retain and enhance its power to discharge that responsibility. Its rewards, both financial and psychological, have been dependent in large measure on the exercise of this function and retention of its leadership.

Unions in general, and the UAW in particular, have challenged management, and thus threatened its authority and status. As we have seen, the UAW has advocated union and government controls over many of the traditional managerial functions of the corporation. This it must do by wresting leadership from the management group. To many executives, therefore, holding the union at arm's length is an important battle in a basic struggle for their survival as a class. General Motors has made a very clear distinction between those who belong to management and those who are the "employees." Management (down to and including the foremen) has been compensated on a salary basis. Foremen have been paid considerably more than the highest rated hourly employees. They have been constantly urged to identify themselves with the management class, and they have been told to differentiate themselves status-wide from the employees (particularly when it comes to joining unions). In short, they are encouraged to look upon their position with respect to the employees as Army officers view their status with respect to enlisted personnel.

Management's basic struggle to preserve its position of leadership in society has been fortified by a deep-seated belief in the righteousness of the cause for which it is fighting. Like the union officials, General Motors management believes it is fighting a battle not only for itself but for what it conceives to be the American way of life.

CHAPTER III

The Resulting Union-Management Relationship

IT is obvious from the facts presented in the preceding chapter that a fundamental disagreement has always existed between the UAW and General Motors in the most vital areas of their relationship. Although the parties have engaged in collective bargaining, each has had a sharply different concept of its proper function and scope.

THE BASIS OF CONFLICT

The conflict of economic and political philosophy has been even more basic. The corporation has stood squarely for freedom of management from government or union regulation. The union has advocated broad social planning through government and labor participation in the economic decision-making of the automotive industry. Underlying these attitudes has been an internal competition for leadership and a determined struggle for power. In almost every labor-management relationship there is some competition for leadership and power between union officials and employers. In the relations between big unions and big corporations this struggle is more pronounced and more vital, not only to the parties but to the nation as well, because their decisions reverberate throughout their organizations, their industries, and the national economy as a whole.

At General Motors the stakes have been high for both management and labor. The UAW officials, for example, have looked upon the corporation's policy of being tough in collective bargaining as an indication of a basically antiunion position. In the minds of UAW officials the corporation's policy of "containing the union" has been merely a tactic designed to strangle it. The whole employee cooperation program of General Motors has been considered a kid-glove method of union busting. Practically all of the UAW officials interviewed indicated that they doubted the good faith of General Motors in collective bargaining. They feared the corporation would kick out the union if it had the power to do so. Since the union leaders believed that the corporation had been trying to bust unions, those leaders have planned and acted as if that were the case.

The union officials have shown the same distrust and suspicion of management's philosophy and social goals. The idea that there has been internal competition within the corporation as a result of the policy of decentralization has been looked upon as a barrage to conceal monopolistic maneuvers. In fact, one official exclaimed, "How could they honestly believe in such lies of that kind?" The militant anti-New Deal orientation of management has been to the union proof of its ultra-reactionary motives. It has been sheer hypocrisy, union officials have said, for an "irresponsible industrial giant" like General Motors to talk about the virtues of free enterprise and the evils of labor monopolies while it spearheaded the forces of "rightist" reaction.

On the corporation side, feelings and beliefs have been equally intense. Management executives have claimed that the union was irresponsible in collective bargaining and politically incapable of abiding by the terms of the contracts it made. Many UAW leaders, they thought, have been striving for only personal prestige and power and have cared little for the interests of the workers they allegedly represented. General Motors executives thought that the UAW ought to be exposed on this score in particular. The UAW has been viewed as almost a mob ruled by dangerous and unscrupulous men who have used force and violence to achieve their selfish ends.

Corporation executives have reacted even more violently to the economic and social philosophy of Reuther. They have implied that his "unioneering" has been just a way-station on the road of his political career. They shuddered at the thought of a man of his calibre and beliefs—as they judged them—ending up in the White House. His program, as planned, has been to them a totalitarian combination of socialism and syndicalism. To them, "state socialism" of the Reuther type has been a cardinal evil. Though they have not referred to Reuther as a Communist or a Nazi, they have implied that some of his ideas have been imported from "east of the Rhine." The basis of these allegations is irrelevant. The important point is that many General Motors executives have believed these things to be true.

We must recognize that these strong beliefs and convictions have existed on both sides. The fears and suspicions of the corporation were raised to a new high by the union's wage-price and "look at the books" policy set forth before and during the 1945–46 strike. The fears and suspicions of the union, on the other hand, were intensified by the extreme and outspoken position of General Motors in pressing for restrictive labor legislation in 1947.

It follows that the most bitter controversies between General Motors and the union have been political as well as economic. When it has come to collective bargaining, the important issues have arisen over the scope and area of collective bargaining—"its proper function." As we have seen, the corporation has wanted to limit the scope of collective bargaining to wages, hours, and working conditions. The union has wanted to broaden it. For example, the corporation has been willing to discuss wages only as wages, while the union has insisted on discussing the relationship of wages to prices, profits, purchasing power, and the broad economic problems of the nation.

A striking feature of this conflict has been that each side has had complete understanding of the thinking, motivation and internal problems of the other. Each party has known where the other stood. The General Motors management has understood fully the objectives of the union. It has had detailed information at all times on the factional fights within the union. The UAW top officials, for their part, have known exactly where General Motors has wanted to go. They have had a good idea of the structure of power within the organization, and they have known the differing viewpoints of various management cliques. In short, there has been substantial agreement between the corporation and the union on the reasons for their basic disagreement on most vital issues.

The struggle between the two parties could hardly have been resolved by better understanding, resulting from sitting around the conference table and exploring mutual interests in "hunting, fishing or the enjoyment of fine music." To be sure, the officials on both sides have been human beings—but they have been playing for blue chips. Each party has well defined motivations growing out of confirmed beliefs which mold their attitudes and actions on the specific issues.

COMPETITION FOR EMPLOYEE AND PUBLIC SUPPORT

As the issues in the GM-UAW relationship have outgrown the common concept of collective bargaining, support from the community has become increasingly important to the success of the program of each. Each side has attempted to line up both the workers and the public behind its position. They and the public have recognized that the issues have importance outside the corporation and outside the industry; thus each side has sought government and public sympathy for its arguments.

The Contest for Workers' Allegiance

In the General Motors plants, as in those in most American industry, there has been a nucleus of active union members who have activated and, for all practical purposes, directed the affairs of the union. Then, too, there has usually been a number of antiunion individualists primarily oriented toward management. Although the majority of General Motors employees have for the most part supported the programs advanced by the active union nucleus, they generally have looked two ways for pay increases, job security, and opportunities for advancement—to the union and to the management. To the extent that management has given them what they wanted, they have been inclined to consider General Motors "not a bad place to work." To the extent that the union has demonstrated its ability to wrest concessions from General Motors, the worker has given the union his backing.

General Motors has considered many employee relations activities appropriately unilateral management functions. Examples of these include the General Motors' suggestion system, sports and social events, employee benefit plans, employee publications, health maintenance, accident prevention, veteran re-employment, morale programs, open-house occasions for families of employees, and other similar activities. In fact, these activities have been under the jurisdiction of a vice president of employee cooperation who has had an organization separate from that of the vice president of personnel, who has been responsible for labor relations. General Motors has maintained a great many direct points of contact with its employees wholly outside the scope of union-management relations. It never has intended to be dependent on the union to find out what is on the employees' minds nor to determine the interests of workers.

The UAW has looked at these activities as subtle devices designed to weaken the union organization. The UAW always has striven to have workers identify their interests and welfare with the union—not with the management or even a possible rival union. The union has had its own employee publications, ball teams, bowling leagues, health maintenance programs, morale activities, and educational programs. It even has had its own employee counselors and veterans' service department.

The corporation and the union have constantly competed to win and hold the loyalty of General Motors employees. In many ways, this competition has made each side do a better job of servicing the employees. On the other hand, it often has resulted in mud slinging, name calling, "hate-management" campaigns or "hate-the-union" tactics, which have served to undermine employee trust in one party or both. Union literature sometimes has described the corporation as controlled by profit-swollen coupon-clippers who have exploited the worker at the expense of the community. Corporation officials periodically have made statements about the integrity and political orientation of the union leaders.

The Play to Influence Public Opinion

Whenever the UAW and General Motors have come to blows, each party has made a determined effort to publicize its viewpoint. Labor relations between UAW and General Motors often have been geared to public relations objectives. Because of the economic leadership of General Motors as a pattern-setter in labor-management relations, each side has felt impelled to mold public opinion. Consequently, the outside manifestations of inner conflict have been revealed quite clearly in the grandstand strategy which each has employed during a showdown.

The negotiations between the UAW and General Motors in the fall of 1945 and the strike which continued throughout the ensuing winter provide good illustrations of this grandstand strategy. Both sides inserted advertisements in newspapers throughout the country. Both acquired radio time on nation-wide hook-ups to present their sides of the controversy. Interviews were given to journalists and writers. Magazines and newspapers carried feature articles about Walter Reuther, C. E. Wilson, the UAW, and the corporation, as well as some of the more spectacular transcripts of the verbal lashings which were so characteristic of the negotiations. The union published its case in attractive form under the imposing title, "Purchasing Power for Prosperity." The corporation countered with pamphlets warning of "Danger on the Production Front."[1] For a time it seemed as though collective bargaining between the parties was confined to the newspapers and the radio!

---

[1] *Danger on the Production Front*, Dec. 18, 1945, pp. 29–34. General Motors also issued a special pamphlet to its management in which it described in detail its methods of keeping the public informed. All in all, between Oct. 4 and Dec. 9, 1945, it published eleven full-page newspaper ads, issued twenty-four press releases, arranged for five special mailings of booklets and copies of newspaper ads to "influential public citizens," and used two or three minute spot radio talks in plant cities.

The union saw to it that it did not come out second best in this publicity contest. It issued cartoons, prepared materials for editors, columnists, and radio commentators. In December, 1945, it called to Detroit a group of "prominent citizens" to review the transcript of the negotiations and make a public report.[2] The union sponsored radio broadcasts and extended open invitations to newspapermen to look over the records of bargaining at any time.

There are differences of opinion as to which side did the more effective job in influencing public opinion. For our purposes, it is sufficient to understand the grandstand strategy as an example of the contest for employee and public support. The propaganda barrages were used as tactical maneuvers in negotiations in much the same way as military commanders use diversionary feints to ambush their opponents. But the main objective of the public relations programs on both sides was to convince people of the righteousness of the respective competing positions, and to keep up morale in the two opposing camps. Although such strategy complicates collective bargaining, it has usually been unavoidable in battles between big corporations and big labor unions.

THE ISSUES IN BARGAINING

When we understand the forces which have motivated the UAW and General Motors in their relationship

---

[2] *Report of the National Citizens Committee on the GM-UAW Dispute* (Detroit: National Citizens Committee, December, 1945). The report supported the union's economic brief. It stated that "the union's request to participate in determination of the wage issue on the basis of full knowledge of the basic wage-price-profit relations is not a 'taking over' of management. . . . . the union . . . . has lifted the level of collective bargaining to a new high by insisting that the advancement of labor's interest shall not be made at the expense of the public."

It is important to remember, however, that much of the talk in bargaining negotiations was for the record. The Reuther group did a much better job in talking for the record than General Motors. In fact, there is doubt that General Motors expected the transcript to be publicized.

with each other, the positions taken by the parties on individual issues in bargaining appear to follow well-defined patterns. Conflict has been greatest over those issues affecting the status of the parties and the balance of power between them. Harmonious relations have been possible when such status and power issues were only remotely involved.

The Controversial Issues

The UAW has advocated equal pay for equal work throughout the industry. The corporation has fought wage equalization, attempting to keep wage-bargaining on an individual company basis. Through bargaining with employers as a group, union leaders have felt they could establish a bridgehead for discussion of broad economic problems in the automotive industry. The corporation has been unconditionally opposed to such industry-wide bargaining not only because it would increase the power of the union but because it represented a step in the direction of what company executives considered a "regimented economy."

The bargaining power of individual employers is often increased if they can make a united stand against a powerful union on an industry-wide basis. General Motors, however, has been powerful enough to deal with the union effectively by itself. In fact, its executives have felt that its bargaining power might be weakened by joining forces with other companies whose labor relations policies were not clearly and consistently defined. Accordingly, General Motors has not participated in industry-wide discussions with the union, even on such questions as production bottlenecks, because the corporation has not wished to set any precedent for industry-wide negotiations. On several occasions during the war and in the summer of 1946, the GM Department of the UAW asked for joint meetings to solve production delays, but the corporation refused to attend these meetings.

Obviously, there has been no meeting of minds between the parties on the issue of union security. When the first UAW-CIO contract was signed, the union was recognized as the bargaining agent for its members only. In 1940, the corporation reluctantly agreed to recognition of the union as the exclusive bargaining agent for all hourly rated employees where the union was certified as representing the majority of workers in the appropriate collective bargaining unit. In 1942, General Motors was directed by the National War Labor Board to grant maintenance of membership. In the negotiations which ended the strike in 1946, it refused to continue the maintenance of membership arrangement and forced the union to agree to the compulsory check-off of dues and assessments of union members as a substitute. Throughout the entire period of their relationship the UAW has pressed for the union shop. Management has vehemently opposed any arrangement to make union membership status a condition of employment, as such a provision would increase the financial strength, and power of the union.

Closely related to the issue of union security has been the vital question of managerial functions. General Motors has been primarily interested in retaining unilateral authority over production planning and pricing, as well as control over employee discipline and production standards. General Motors has appeared willing at all times to stand a strike to combat major encroachments by unions into the area of traditional management functions. The UAW has agreed to management rights clauses in the contract with notable lack of enthusiasm. From the outset of the bargaining relationship, there has never been a meeting of minds on this vital issue.

Another controversial issue has been whether sick-pay plans, pension programs and similar employee welfare schemes came within the area of collective bargaining. Many persons within the UAW have felt that employee security measures ought to be provided by a broad government social security program, rather than by collective bargaining with individual employers or particular industries. In 1947 they felt that it was virtually impossible to make gains along these lines in the near future in view of the antagonistic attitude of Congress. Their only alternative, therefore, was to press for employee welfare programs by bargaining with employers. Here again the UAW has met with continued resistance from General Motors.

The corporation has refused to broaden the area of collective bargaining to include measures of this kind. It has wanted to retain its right to establish such programs on a unilateral basis, as it has done in the case of salaried employees, if it went in for them at all. Under no circumstances has it wanted any kind of jointly administered program. It has resisted the idea of making employee participation in such plans a condition of employment.

Finally, there has been no evidence of common thinking on the issue of the guaranteed annual wage. General Motors has made detailed studies of the extent to which employment stabilization might be possible in its plants as well as the costs involved in guaranteeing wages when work is not available. As a practical matter, General Motors has decided that a rigid annual wage guarantee for GM workers is an impossibility. The UAW has advocated the annual wage, but has not pressed very hard for adoption of the principle in union contracts. There has been a difference of opinion, furthermore, among UAW officers as to whether the union should press for employment guarantees through collective bargaining.

Many union leaders have felt that employment and income guarantees should be made by government rather than by individual employers. Annual wage, accordingly, has not been an issue on which there were clear-cut positions on both sides. It is certain that the annual wage principle could not be applied in the automotive industry without far-reaching production and sales planning on an industry-wide basis. This issue is thus tied up with the broader problem of industry-wide bargaining and joint economic planning. The opposition of General Motors to union encroachments in this area, as we have pointed out, has been extremely strong.

Areas of Agreement

Up to this point, we have emphasized the areas of conflict between General Motors and the UAW. These areas have been, of course, much broader than the areas of common interest. Yet, many issues have been handled satisfactorily through collective bargaining.

One of the most important provisions in the agreements between General Motors and UAW, both in the master contract and in local supplementary agreements, has related to seniority. When the union was first recognized in 1937, there was agreement that, with minor exceptions, lay-offs and re-employment would be made on the basis of length of service, provided the employees possessed the minimum qualifications necessary for performance of the jobs to which they were assigned. Management agreed to the application of seniority rules with few qualifications. As time went on, straight seniority was applied more rigidly to lay-offs and generally accepted without question by both sides. There have been, of course, long and protracted bargaining conferences over the application of seniority by occupational groups, departments or plants. Endless discussions have developed over whether or not an employee had sufficient ability to perform a job. Also, there has been bargaining about the seniority status of veterans, of workers transferred to other plants or companies during the war, of women employees, of temporary versus permanent lay-offs, of bumping, and other matters—all headaches for both parties. There has been joint concern in trying to alleviate them. For the most part, such problems have been settled by bargaining at the plant and corporation levels.

The corporation has opposed the use of straight seniority as a basis for promotion and transfer, holding that transfers and promotions should be made on the basis of merit and ability as determined by management. The union has had many complaints on this score and has wanted much more weight given to seniority than the corporation has been willing to concede. A good many cases of individual promotion, in which management has claimed that merit and ability outweighed seniority, have been carried to the umpire. The corporation has won many of these cases which has disturbed the union officials. The corporation likewise has been disturbed when the umpire ruled that seniority should apply. On the other hand, since the details of seniority have not affected vitally the balance of power between the parties, mutual agreement has been possible at least on the broad principles governing the application of seniority to promotions.

The parties have bargained effectively on such things as working hours, night shift premiums, provisions governing leaves of absence, the number and function of shop committeemen, vacations with pay, and similar matters falling within the scope of conditions of employment. The corporation has thought that such matters were proper subjects for joint determination through collective bargaining. The union, furthermore, has recognized that its members take a great deal of interest in shop regulations.

It has been successful in getting some concessions from management in this area. During the war most of these issues were settled by directive orders of the National War Labor Board. When the union could not get concessions from the corporation on these issues, it passed them on to the NWLB in an attempt to secure a better settlement. This procedure was largely the result of suspension of free collective bargaining during the war, rather than an indication of basic differences between the parties. When the NWLB faded out of the picture, the parties were able to resolve these issues through collective bargaining.

Common Concern over Contract Administration

There has also been a substantial meeting of minds in the general administration of the agreement. Developing workable grievance machinery covering more than 100 plants and 300,000 employees has been in itself a tremendous undertaking. It has required an understanding on the part of thousands of foremen and union stewards not only of the terms of the agreement but also of its various interpretations. It has called for face-to-face, day-to-day relationships between union and management rank and file in the midst of technological and managerial changes in plants, and in the heat of political rivalries and factional disputes within local unions. These relationships have been strained by the drastic organizational upheavals necessitated by thorough-going conversion of plants to war production and reconversion to peacetime manufacturing. Yet, the record of UAW and General Motors in the area of contract administration has been, on the whole, an exceptionally successful one. There have been stoppages and unauthorized strikes, but fewer of them by far than in most of the other companies in the industry.

In some General Motors plants, the relationships between the local managements and local unions have been remarkably effective. Local agreements on the details of such matters as seniority have been worked out to the complete satisfaction of both parties; grievances have been settled in an orderly and prompt fashion.

There have been several reasons for the apparent harmony which has existed in some plants of the corporation while conflict at the top levels has remained so pronounced. First, the parties at the local level have been concerned with contract administration. They have not been engaged in the troublesome agreement-making and policy-determining process. The area of collective relationships has been specifically defined for them in the corporation-wide agreement; their scope of decision-making has been limited to plant problems and day-to-day operations. Both sides, at the lower levels, therefore, have tended to look upon their situation this way: "Here is the agreement which 'the big shots' have negotiated in Detroit. Whether it is good or bad, we can't change it. Let's make the best of the situation and settle our local problems as peacefully as possible." Second, the issues to be settled at the plant level have usually been practical shop problems that could usually be solved by laying easily ascertainable facts out on the table. In cases of this kind, the establishment of principles or the power status of the parties has not been involved. Third, in cases where good relations have been maintained there are usually men on both sides who have unusual ability in handling human relations. This had made for mutual respect and confidence on both sides. Fourth, in such situations the local plant relationships, as a rule, have not been plagued by pronounced factional cleavages within the local union. The local union officials have enjoyed relatively secure status as leaders in their organizations. Finally, both sides often have felt that they would rather settle their differences in their own plant than get either the International or the Detroit office of the corporation embroiled in local issues.

In some plants, on the other hand, constant tension and conflict have existed between the local unions and the plant management. In others, the relationship has seemed to alternate, being quite harmonious at times and fraught with controversy at others. Within the General Motors setup, there have been, consequently, many different shades of local union-management relationships— some outstandingly stable, some quite unstable, and many in-between.

The slogan of the General Motors executives in settlement of local grievances might be set forth as follows: "Be tough, but fair, and don't deviate from the letter of the 'little gray book.' " To top General Motors officials this has been a cardinal principle; to the management rank and file it has been the law. The policy of the UAW-General Motors Department, which has coordinated contract administration matters for the union, has also been to insist on strict adherence to the contract although it sometimes has deplored narrow and legalistic interpretations.

The steps in the grievance procedure have been as follows: The employee in a plant first took up his grievance with his foreman who attempted to adjust it. The employee might then request the foreman to call in the union district committeeman or steward. The grievance was reduced to writing and, if not adjusted at this step (Step 1), it was referred to a member of the union shop committee. The shop committee met periodically with a standing committee of the plant management. Grievances were discussed in these meetings. If the grievance was not settled at this level (Step 2) within a specified number of days, it was sent to the UAW regional office (usually to a field representative of the General Motors

Department of the UAW) who might then submit it to an appeal board (Step 3). If not disposed at this step, it could be submitted (after screening[3] by the General Motors Department of UAW) for final settlement by the impartial umpire (Step 4).

Approximately 35,000 written grievances have been filed by the union each year in General Motors plants. Nearly half of the grievances have been settled in the first step; about nine-tenths disposed of at the plant level, and less than 1 per cent referred to the umpire. From a technical standpoint this system has worked well and efficiently. Most grievances have been settled reasonably close to their origin and time lags in settlement have not been great. The UAW, however, has insisted that General Motors has stalled deliberately and has made it very difficult to process grievances rapidly. The corporation sometimes has made the same charge against the union.

The keystone of the procedure has been the umpire system. The authority of the umpire has been carefully, specifically and narrowly defined in the master agreement. He has had power to rule on claims of violation of most of the sections of the master contract or local supplementary agreements. He could also review such things as disciplinary action on discharges for violation of shop rules. This power to review disciplinary action cases has

---

[3] In 1944 the International Executive Board created a Board of Review Committee of nine regional directors. The purpose of this board has been to screen out grievances which had little merit. The Board of Review system has operated in the following way:

Grievances which had been appealed to the umpire but which had not yet been placed on the umpire's docket were examined by a committee on the GM Department staff and cases which seemed to be of dubious merit were sent to a Board of Review made up of three appropriate members of the Board of Review Committee. This Board of Review could decide whether or not the cases should be carried further and processed to the umpire. The Boards of Review were quite successful and resulted in considerable economy of GM Department staff's time.

been delegated to the umpire by General Motors. The authority and responsibility for maintaining discipline of employees in the plant has remained solely in the hands of management. The umpire has not had power to modify the agreement in any way, to establish or change any wage rate, nor to rule on any dispute regarding production standards. As an umpire he has been expected to stand behind the plate and call "balls or strikes"—that's all. It is interesting to note that the first two umpires under the GM agreement tended to look upon their job as one of educating the parties as well as passing judgment on individual cases. Their aim was to encourage on both sides a better appreciation and understanding of the positive and constructive features of good collective bargaining relationships. Their main purpose was to resolve issues and conflicts and to suggest solutions of some basic problems in human relationships. The last two umpires have been required to "call the shots" and to leave the job of evolving principles to the parties. The umpire has not been supposed to solve a problem—he has been there to pass judgment on each case solely on the basis of the evidence presented to him by the parties.

Through the years the decisions of the umpire have helped to build up a body of "common law" applicable to grievance settlement within General Motors. Copies of the umpire's decisions have been circulated by the corporation to 12,000 members of the General Motors management, and by the union to its thousands of local officers and committeemen. On both sides "shop lawyers" had to become acquainted with the fine points and technicalities of this accumulation of important precedents. The result has been to introduce order and consistency into the far-flung operations of the grievance machinery. At the same time, it brought about a kind of dehydration of the human relationships between the parties. The grievances which could be settled by procedure were resolved, but there may have been no effective drainage system for the multitude of beefs and frustrations which are not covered by contract. • This has been one reason why there has often been a great deal of employee dissatisfaction in many plants. There simply has been no provision for attacking some very fundamental human relations problems.

This grievance procedure has been essentially a system of rules. A certain amount of cooperation has been evident in the efforts at the top of both sides to require rigid adherence to these rules throughout their respective organizations. The establishment of precedents and principles has been all-important. Both sides have been apt to think more in terms of technicalities than of equities in human relations. The procedure has not been so dependent, as it is in many other companies, on personalities, for the discretion allowed to individuals has been rather narrowly circumscribed by rules and precedents. It has provided, however, a cold and mechanistic kind of protection of individual employee rights.

Why have both parties cooperated in making this legalistic grievance machinery work effectively? The answers to this question are easily found. The settlement of grievances under the contract has affected only remotely the status and the balance of power between the corporation and the union. In important respects the procedure has strengthened the hand of top officials of both sides. A rigid grievance procedure has made it easier for the corporation to control the decisions and actions of management's rank and file. Thousands of plant managers, department superintendents and foremen have been dealing with union representatives on a day-to-day basis. Many of them have been inexperienced in labor-relations, and some were bound to make mistakes. The existence of a system of rules has made it easier for top company officials to locate quickly those spots where local management has been "off base." Furthermore, it has been easier to train local managers and foremen to follow specific rules than to educate them to use discretion in dealing with their counterparts on the union side. In an organization the size of General Motors, this has been a matter of great practical importance.

The top union officers have also had a stake in the procedure. Local unions have been often in a state of upheaval as a result of factional cleavages, internal battles for power, and political alignments. The authority and power of UAW's top leadership has been more tenuous than that of the top command of many other large mass production unions. A grievance procedure based upon rigid rules and precedents has had a stabilizing effect on the administration of internal union affairs. By insisting upon adherence to the letter of a contract, top union officials could often check-mate possible rebellions of insurgent local unions. The referral of a critical case to the umpire for adjudication, furthermore, often has taken heat off the international officers.[4] Thus the grievance

---

[4] In his brief submitted to the U.S. Senate Committee on Labor and Public Welfare on Feb. 21, 1947, Walter Reuther praised the GM umpire system in glowing terms. Part of his statement read:

"For almost seven years the General Motors employees have had an opportunity to get action and if necessary a final decision on their grievances without having to force the issue by going on strike. We are proud of the way in which they have used that opportunity. Some unauthorized 'quickie' strikes have occurred during these seven years, but the man days lost have been lower at General Motors than at almost any other large industrial company. Mr. C. E. Wilson, President of the Corporation, has himself attested to that fact. In the few 'wildcat' stoppages which have occurred because of momentary outbursts of anger or impatience, our union was able in a matter of a few hours or at the most a day or two, to persuade the employees to return to work. The primary reason we were able to do this is because the umpire machinery was in existence and we could convince the employees that they did not have to strike in order to obtain a fair disposition of their grievances."

procedure in general and the umpire system in particular have made it easier for the union to hold its rank and file in line.

The UAW, although it has supported and proudly defended the umpire system, has not been sold on its formal and legalistic characteristics. In the first place, the rigid nature of the umpire system has made it difficult for the union to broaden day-to-day collective bargaining to cover problems of the workers which did not come squarely under this or that provision in the contract. Secondly, the union officials have charged that the corporation sometimes has taken advantage of "technicalities," refusing to recognize the basic human relations problems involved. Finally, the union has won only a small proportion of the cases which have reached the umpire. Some cases have had to be appealed to the umpire for political reasons irrespective of merit. The rulings in such cases which favored the corporation often created resentment and pressure against the umpire system within the ranks of the union.

The corporation has looked upon the grievance machinery as a great achievement in collective bargaining and as an effective stabilizing device in management-union relations. General Motors executives for the most part have thought that the formality and semi-legal nature of the umpire system were its greatest assets. In their opinion, it has tended to keep the management-union relationship "on the beam"; it has made "contract-stretching" by the union more difficult; it has been a good device for confining collective bargaining to its proper scope.

In the minds of the corporation executives who have compared this union-management relationship with the old open shop days, General Motors has come a long way in promoting good and sound collective bargaining. In the eyes of the union leaders, who have measured the existing situation in terms of their long-range goals of industrial democracy, it has represented only a modest first step. To the public at large it has represented progress under difficult and trying circumstances.

WAGES AND THE STRIKE OF 1945-46

Despite all of the publicity about the subject, wages as such have not been one of the major bones of contention between the parties up to 1947 for several reasons. First, both parties agreed that wages were a proper subject for collective bargaining. Second, employment, technological efficiency, production, prices and wages were rising during the ten year period of bargaining. The economic environment, in other words, made it possible for the union to press successfully for wage increases. Average wage rates nearly doubled between 1936 and 1947. Third, during the war the final authority on such matters rested with the government. Consequently during the emergency the UAW was in reality bargaining with the government on wages rather than with General Motors.

After V-J Day the most bitter and prolonged strike in the history of the automotive industry occurred. A strike was called in November, 1945 which was not ended until February, 1946. This controversy actually centered on the issue of the scope of collective bargaining, not on the issue of wages.[5]

After the President lifted the government restriction on wage increases on August 18, 1945, Walter Reuther of the UAW-General Motors Department addressed a demand to General Motors Corporation for a general 30

---

[5] It is beyond the scope of this study to trace the story of this strike or even to give a complete statement of all of the issues involved. Our purpose is merely to outline the main focal points of controversy and the manner in which they were finally resolved.

per cent wage increase. This demand was based upon an expected decline in weekly earnings resulting from a reduction in the standard work-week from forty-eight hours to forty hours with consequent elimination of overtime pay. The purpose of this demand was maintenance of wartime earnings on peacetime production in the interest of assuring purchasing power.

The union made it clear that this wage increase had to be met without a corresponding increase in prices. The union anticipated that whatever settlement was reached in General Motors would set a wage pattern. If prices were to be increased as wages were pushed up, the workers would be paid off in inflated dollars. The UAW, therefore, tried to exert pressure in two directions at once; first upon the corporation for wage increases, and second upon the government and General Motors to keep the lid on prices. The UAW wanted to establish this principle of wage increases without price increases as a yardstick to guide the reconversion wage policy of the nation.

In its bargaining conferences the union contended that General Motors could grant a 30 per cent increase in wages without raising prices. At the same time the union indicated that it would accept less than 30 per cent providing it was established that the corporation could not carry the load without increasing prices. This principle of linking a wage increase to a company's price policy was a new departure in collective bargaining in the mass production industries.

The corporation rejected the 30 per cent demand as "unreasonable." It then made counter-proposals involving wages and hours which were not acceptable to the union. At the same time it refused to consider the issue of prices in negotiations. The real controversy between the parties then centered on the question of whether prices were a proper subject for collective bargaining. Union spokesmen contended that prices and profits were of vital interest to the union and to the public, that they were tied to the wage issue, and that the UAW had a right to bargain about them. General Motors contended that prices and profits were the corporation's business. The corporation's executives suggested to the UAW officials that they drop their "socialistic ideas," get down on the level of "just representing the UAW people" and talk about wages.[6] The corporation made it clear that it would discuss only wages, hours, or working conditions with the union. In accordance with the basic corporation policy, it would not under any circumstances bring profits and prices into the scope of negotiations. The union contended that this position constituted refusal to bargain within the meaning of the National Labor Relations Act.

The controversy grew sharper when the union, pressing the corporation for proof of alleged inability to pay, asked for "a look at the books." At this point the corporation charged that the union was spurred on by "radical ideology" in making prices and ability to pay rather than wages per se the prime issue. When a government fact-finding board was appointed to pass judgment on the dispute, General Motors withdrew from the proceedings as soon as that board announced that ability-to-pay would be regarded as one of the factors relevant to the wage issue. General Motors told the Fact Finding Board that the corporation would not participate in the proceedings as long as the "revolutionary . . . . proposal" and "radical

---

[6] The first proposal, made by C. E. Wilson in a press conference October 19, was that the work-week be extended from forty to forty-five or forty-eight hours. On November 7, 1945, the corporation offered 8 to 10 per cent wage increases. On November 8, 1945, the corporation refused to offer even 1 per cent with the agreement that it would not seek price increases based on the wage increase. Later on the corporation offered thirteen and one-half cents and finally settled at eighteen and one-half cents but refused to make any no-price-rise commitment.

ideology" of the union were given credence by the board. The corporation maintained this stand despite President Truman's statements (December 21, December 27) and the recommendations of the Fact Finding Board that the economic facts be included in arbitrating the dispute.

Throughout this struggle the union made a determined effort to lift the wage issue out of the traditional area of collective bargaining in order to press for a broad program of wage-price adjustment for the reconversion period. Such tactics were consistent with the objective of joint planning in basic industries as had been advocated for years by its officials responsible for dealing with General Motors.

The UAW, in effect, made a frontal attack on one of the most carefully fortified and staunchly defended positions of the corporation—exclusive managerial authority to determine prices and production policies. On this issue General Motors won a decisive victory. Although a wage increase of eighteen and one-half cents per hour was granted, it conformed to the pattern set in negotiations with the steel industry and the two other large automobile companies. The matter of prices, profits, and "ability to pay" was left exclusively in General Motors' hands. Later in 1946 the corporation secured permission from the government to increase the price of its cars.

The union had gained ground in its public relations. Its fight for wage increases without price raises had an appeal to many non-labor consumers feeling the pinch of inflation. Throughout the entire labor movement there was increased awareness in the difference between real wages and money wages. This can be attributed in part to UAW's position in the strike. After the OPA program ended in the summer of 1946, prices and profits soared to new heights. Money wage increases received by mass production workers were quickly wiped out by sharp increases in the cost of living. Regardless of whether they agreed with Reuther's arithmetic, a large segment of labor and the public was impressed with his basic argument that some conscious and determined effort must be made to keep wages and prices in proper relationship. Reuther's insistence upon linking wage increases to company price policies, no matter how distasteful to General Motors, also won him great support among progressive groups throughout the nation. Reuther was successful in the sense that he made wage-price relationships in basic industries a national issue.

Both union and management spokesmen seemed to be agreed afterwards that the strike, which lasted more than three months, could have been settled in a much shorter time if the UAW had been content to press for wage increases without bringing prices or ability to pay into the negotiations. The course of this strike, consequently, has fortified our conviction that the basic controversies between the parties have centered around the scope of collective bargaining relationships and the status and rights of the parties rather than on such issues as rates of pay and working conditions.[7]

---

[7] Detailed statements of the corporation and union positions in the 1945–46 strike can be found in the following:

Walter P. Reuther, "The Challenge of Peace," *International Postwar Problems*, II, No. 2 (April, 1945).

Purchasing Power for Prosperity (Detroit: GM Department, UAW-CIO, November, 1945).

H. W. Anderson, *General Motors' Reply to UAW-CIO Brief* (Detroit: General Motors Corporation, 1945).

"Controversy between General Motors and the United Automobile Workers," *Congressional Record*, 79th Congress, 1st session (1945). Remarks of Senator James E. Murray on Oct. 24, 1945, and of Senator Glen H. Taylor on Nov. 6, 1945.

Here Is the Issue (Detroit: General Motors Corporation, 1946).

W. G. Merritt, "Statement in behalf of General Motors before the Fact-Finding Board," *General Motors News Release*, Dec. 28, 1945.

In March, 1946 the parties negotiated an agreement for a two-year period. The new agreement contained practically all of the basic provisions of the prior contract which had been terminated in December, 1945. The main changes were incorporation of the eighteen and one-half cent wage increase and the substitution of a "maintenance of dues" clause (check-off of dues of union members) for the maintenance of membership provision which had been put in the earlier agreement by direction of the National War Labor Board. Provision was made, in addition, for either party to open the agreement on wages and other "economic issues" on May 31, 1947. Either party could request negotiations on such issues after March 19, 1947.

THE 1947 BARGAINING ON ECONOMIC ISSUES

The negotiations between General Motors and the UAW in 1947 were simple and peaceful compared with those of the preceding year. In the first place, the contract could be opened only on economic issues. The more troublesome issues involving the status of the parties were frozen for a two-year period in the 1946 agreement. In the second place, the pattern of wage and economic issues in the basic industries was already being formulated in the steel and electrical manufacturing industries where agreements expired in the last week of April, a month before the GM-UAW contract was reopenable. It was obvious therefore that in the 1947 round of demands the

---

President's Fact-Finding Board in the General Motors Case, *Official Transcript of Proceedings*, Dec. 28, 1945. Walter Reuther's extemporaneous remarks in response to the W. G. Merritt statement.

Official Transcript of the GM-UAW negotiations proceedings in October, November, December, 1945 (Detroit: UAW-CIO, 1946).

Victor G. Reuther, "Responsibility of the General Motors Corporation to GM Employees and to the Nation"; an address broadcast Jan. 15, 1946 (Detroit: Education Dept., UAW-CIO, 1946).

Victor G. Reuther, "The Next Fifty Years," *Detroit*, June, 1946.

UAW would be following rather than leading as it had a year earlier.[8]

In negotiations which started in March the UAW asked General Motors for a twenty-three and one-half cent wage increase, jointly administered but company financed social security and old age retirement plans, and a forty hour pay guarantee for all employees during any week in which they were called for work. The wage increase was demanded because of the sharp rise in cost of living which followed the abolition of most government price controls. This was justified, in the view of the union, on the basis of the corporation's ability to pay. In requesting the weekly pay guarantee the UAW hoped to take a first step toward the guaranteed annual wage. The social security demands were a logical response to the precedents set by John L. Lewis a year earlier, the postwar feelings of insecurity on the part of the workers, and a political environment unfavorable to broadening the federal social insurance program.

From the outset it was apparent that General Motors would give a wage increase in line with patterns to be established throughout the mass production industries. The prospects for high production and good earnings throughout 1947 were most favorable. The corporation, however, was not prone to agree to any new principles of pay guarantee. In particular, it did not want to broaden

---

[8] The parties apparently recognized that in 1947 they might be conforming to rather than setting wage patterns. For example, the 1946 agreement contained this interesting provision:

"If during the course of negotiations between March 19, 1947, and May 31, 1947, the corporation shall make an offer of a general wage increase *equal to the general wage pattern which has been established in the automobile industry prior to or during such period,* the corporation may place such offer into effect during the period, if acceptable to the union, on the date such pattern was established but in no event prior to March 19, 1947." Agreement between General Motors Corporation and the UAW-CIO, March 19, 1946, paragraph 153, italics inserted.

the area of collective bargaining by agreement on any kind of jointly administered welfare or insurance plan.

The bargaining power of General Motors this time was far superior to that of the UAW. The GM workers, who had lost over three months of work the previous year, were in no mood to strike for the purpose of trying to "set another pattern." In addition, Congress was considering restrictive labor legislation. In the light of these considerations, General Motors was in a strong position to hold firm on the principles which it deemed important to the corporation's future.

Early in the bargaining negotiations, General Motors offered a wage increase of ten cents an hour to be effective for a four-months period, after which the wage issue could be reopened. This offer was made not only to the UAW but also to the United Electrical Radio and Machine Workers (CIO) and the United Rubber Workers (CIO) with which the corporation was also bargaining.[9] Two days after this offer the corporation reached an agreement with the UE providing for an eleven and one-half cent wage increase, plus another three and one-half cents in the form of six paid holidays and some other minor economic items—a total increase of fifteen cents. The agreement was made for a full year. The UE's social security demands, roughly similar to those of the UAW, were to remain subjects for discussion and negotiations.

The UE settlement came as a bombshell to the Reuther forces. In the opinion of the Reuther group, the UE had sold out to the corporation by backing down on the social security issues, and "artificially" got in the spotlight for the moment as pattern-setter in the basic indus-

---

[9] The UAW represented most of the auto, truck, and engine plants. The UER&MW and the URW represented a small number of home appliance and accessory plants, comprising only about 30,000 and 3,500 General Motors employees respectively.

tries. This entire situation was particularly distasteful to the Reuther group because the pattern was first set with General Motors. It was established by an electrical workers' union which ironically represented only about one-tenth the number of GM workers that were represented by the UAW. The Reuther group was further aggravated by the UE's lead because that union was dominated by the left-wing elements—Reuther's arch enemies in the labor movement. After the General Motors settlement, the UE set the pattern directly in the electrical manufacturing industry by securing an agreement with the Westinghouse Manufacturing Company similar to that negotiated with General Motors. General Motors then offered the UAW the same settlement as the UE had negotiated, to be effective immediately. It gave the union thirteen days to make up its mind. The UAW turned it down as not enough and termed the UE agreement an "artificial pattern." But the UAW was under pressure. Every day it held out its members were losing the immediate benefit of the proposed increase in pay.

By the end of the week the United Steelworkers (CIO) had reached agreement with the United States Steel Corporation on an increase aggregating fifteen cents and a new over-all contract which included many noteworthy gains. The steel settlement granted twelve and one-half cents for a general wage increase, and an additional two and one-half cents for other economic items, including a severance pay provision. United States Steel also agreed to a joint study looking toward the establishment of a life, accident, health, medical and hospital insurance plan. Its president, Benjamin Fairless, indicated in a statement that there was agreement on the principle of a social insurance plan, and that it would be put into effect as soon as methods of financing and administration could be agreed upon.

Recognizing that fifteen cents was the upper limit, Reuther then proposed to General Motors three means of paying the fifteen cent increase: first, as a twelve and one-half cent increase with two and one-half cents applied to a social security and hospitalization plan; second, as a thirteen cent increase with two cents applied to an old age retirement plan; and third, as a flat fifteen cent wage increase. Obviously, he was out to get a better deal than the UE and to gain, if possible, some of the very favorable concessions secured in steel by Philip Murray. General Motors, by this time in an excellent bargaining position, in effect replied: "Take the UE terms by the first of May or we will withdraw our offer." Reuther proposed arbitration; the corporation refused, contending the issues should and could be settled by direct collective bargaining. The UAW then accepted General Motors' terms. It secured a wage increase of eleven and one-half cents, six paid holidays for which it didn't ask, some minor improvements in the vacation plan, and a tabling of its basic social security and pay guarantee demands.

The 1947 showing of the UAW in General Motors was far short of its spectacular demonstration in the previous year. In the parlance of the automotive industry, General Motors "pulled the rug under Reuther" by making a bargain (consonant with its basic principles) with a rival union group—the UE. The more spectacular general union gains in 1947 were made in negotiations with other large corporations. The United Steelworkers, for example, in negotiations with United States Steel established the principle of severance pay and approached a meeting of minds on a pension plan. The UAW forces in the Ford plants, furthermore, later reached agreement on a comprehensive pension plan.

In fact, in 1947 the Ford negotiations were perhaps on a par with the General Motors negotiations in setting the economic and industrial relations patterns for the automotive industry.[10]

THE BALANCE OF POWER IN 1947

Throughout most of the ten-year period of bargaining with General Motors the UAW has been on the offensive. After establishing itself in the plants in the late thirties, it fought for and secured wage increases plus other economic concessions for its members. It wrested a measure of control over employment conditions from management through the rigid application of seniority rules. In conjunction with the corporation there was established a system of industrial jurisprudence and formalized machinery for settlement of grievances. The union, in effect, forced General Motors to make basic and far-reaching changes in its concepts and methods of handling labor relations.

After 1940 the UAW pressed consistently, though generally unsuccessfully, for industry-wide bargaining, for pooling of manufacturing capacity for war production, for making price policy a subject of joint union-management determination, and for jointly administered company-financed employee security programs. During most of the time it was given encouragement by friendly government officials. The general government attitude was favorable to the cause of organized labor. For the most part, General Motors was in fact waging a defensive battle against the inroads of both unions and the government.

By the middle of 1946, however, the balance of power shifted in the corporation's favor. General Motors

---

[10] The extent to which the pattern-setting function for the automotive industry has shifted to Ford, as a result of the jointly established pension plan, is difficult to predict at this time. However, it will be remembered that Ford did not set a pattern as a result of its recognition of the Foreman's Association of America. Nor did Ford's granting of substantial union security to the UAW have very wide following in the industry.

came out on top in the strike of 1945-46. The UAW attained none of its basic objectives. In 1947 the corporation forced the UAW to settle on terms established in bargaining with another union which was really a political rival of the Reuther group and outside the automotive industry. The return of a Republican Congress had also shifted the weight of government to the side of management. The Taft-Hartley Law was passed by a Congress which strongly advocated curbs on the power of labor unions. The Reuther group, as well as other large union groups in the labor movement, was on the defensive.

Yet the balance of power could easily be shifted again in the opposite direction. The Reuther group was strongly entrenched in the General Motors plants, as well as in the labor movement as a whole. A business recession coupled with a change of attitude in Washington could easily result in a shift of power to the union side. Although on the defensive in 1947, the UAW in General Motors was holding fast. There could be little doubt that it was there to stay.

SUMMARY

From our analysis of the labor-management relationship between General Motors and the UAW these conclusions may be drawn:

The areas of actual and potential conflict between the corporation and the union have been greater by far than the areas of accord. The union-management relationship has been reasonably effective, however, in disposing of issues which both parties have agreed came within the scope of collective bargaining. These issues have included such matters as working conditions, seniority rules, and machinery for settlement of grievances. Considering the size and complexity of the corporation's operations and the size and internal political problems of the union, these issues have been disposed of with remarkable efficiency and uniformity in the day-to-day process of bargaining. In this area, great progress has been made under trying circumstances.

Both parties have made a determined effort to live up to the letter of the contracts made between them; both have been "tough" in their dealings with one another; both have given greater weight to the establishment of precedents and principles than to individual problems and equities. General Motors has preferred this legalistic approach to contract administration. The UAW has appeared to accept it only because it was unable to force the corporation to follow any different course.

The fundamental conflict between the parties has resulted from their sharply differing concepts and beliefs on what collective bargaining should include rather than from any inability to settle issues which came within the scope of collective bargaining as conceived by the corporation. General Motors has looked upon collective bargaining as a means of limiting negotiations with unions to the area of wages, hours and conditions of employment. The UAW has attempted to expand the scope of collective bargaining in order to give labor a voice in matters of policy and administration in the automotive industry.

The union officials dealing with General Motors have seemed to be convinced that full production and full employment in the automotive industry could be assured only if social controls were exerted over big business enterprises such as this corporation. These leaders have advocated that the union, and if necessary the government, participate in shaping the major policies of General Motors and the automotive industry to ensure protection of the economic interests of both workers and the public. The UAW has identified its fight for intelligent planning with a crusade to usher in a new era of security and opportunity for the common man. Its ultimate goal has been the transformation of an "anarchic economy into a rational industrial society."

The insistence by the corporation on protection of its managerial functions at all costs has its roots in the conviction that the union has been striving to undermine the authority, leadership and power of management, and has as its ultimate objective the destruction of private enterprise. Destruction of private enterprise, the corporation has held, would destroy individual freedom and wreck industrial efficiency. General Motors, accordingly, has identified its tough policy of keeping the union at arm's length with an ideological battle for preservation of free enterprise and the "American way of life."

The conflict between the corporation and the union stems from a power struggle between those forces fighting for unrestricted freedom for private enterprise and those forces advocating some form of planning in the economy. These opposing economic and political philosophies have been rooted deeply in the attitudes, beliefs, and convictions of the parties. They have been related to the preservation of status and authority, and the struggle for leadership between union officials representing workers as a class and corporation executives representing management as a class.

This power struggle has explained to a large degree the motivations on both the management and the union side. These motivations have constituted the two sides of the mold which has shaped the relationship existing between them and the positions taken by the parties on nearly all issues.

Although there has been evidence of stability in this labor-management relationship, it has been like that of an armed truce rather than a permanent peace treaty. Issues in collective bargaining have been decided by the parties within the context of a struggle for power. Wage determination, for example, has been and is likely to be approached primarily on the basis of its expected implications on the status positions of the parties and the balance of power between them. The very size and financial strength of General Motors has made it the most logical target for UAW strategy. It has been one of the principal pattern-makers in labor-management relations for the entire automotive industry, and, to some extent, for the economy of the nation as a whole.

In order to make gains in the field of collective bargaining and to press for economic planning in the industry, therefore, the UAW must continually try to get General Motors to set the pace. Conversely, as long as General Motors is "tough" and follows a policy of containing unions and restricting the scope of their activities, the UAW can expect the same kind of resistance from many other quarters in the industry.

Studebaker and the UAW

PART THREE

CHAPTER IV

Background and Approach to Union-Management Relations

STUDEBAKER Corporation, leading "independent" of the automotive industry, has not had a major strike in its company history, stretching back nearly a century. No authorized work stoppage against Studebaker has been called in years of collective bargaining by Local 5, UAW-CIO or its predecessor. A national magazine highlighted its Studebaker report by emphasizing the company's "glass-smooth labor relations."[1] Behind this outstanding record of industrial peace lies a fascinating story. A story made all the more significant by the size of the company (12,000 workers), the mass production character of the industry, and the militancy of the bargaining union, UAW-CIO.

INDUSTRIAL PEACE

When we analyze the reasons for this industrial peace we find policies and motivations on each side of the bargaining table, which, while not identical or directed towards the same goals, mesh with each other. The result has been effective, stable union-company relations which have weathered both war and postwar dislocations without any essential change in character.

Collective bargaining at Studebaker has been carried on for many years within the framework of the labor re-

---

[1] "Studebaker," *Life*, XXI, No. 12 (Sept. 16, 1946), 66.

lations atmosphere established at such focal points as General Motors, Chrysler, and Ford. But the imprint of the automotive industry pattern has been significantly altered in important regards at Studebaker. The contrast in industrial peace is one good index of this.

When union and company bargain at Studebaker the focus of attention is on local issues.[2] Without the broad industry pattern as a guide, particularly on money matters, the bargaining picture might be quite different. But granted the benchmarks set by the pattern, which both sides accept, company and union devote their bargaining energies to the achievement of a balance of power that has been rewarding in different ways to each side. The company has not acted towards the union as though it possessed the concentrated economic power and leadership in the economy of the General Motors Corporation. The local union has not retaliated with a corresponding marshalling of forces in emulation of the GM Department of the UAW. It makes a difference.

BACKGROUND OF CORPORATION LABOR POLICY

An understanding of the company's labor policy depends upon a knowledge of the factors underlying this policy. Briefly these background factors are: (1) in recent years the company has trod rough financial ground

---

[2] This study is based upon extensive interviews with management officials and union members and officers of both the local and international union. One of the most fruitful sources of information was the verbatim, unedited minutes of negotiating and grievance handling meetings between union and management. This record gave deep insight into the way union and company react to each other in actual face-to-face relations. This verbatim record does not have the defect of making it necessary to cut through rationalizations or overcome fallible memory of a person being interviewed. The corporation generously made the record available with union concurrence. Copies of these minutes are made for the union as a standard procedure so that both union and company will have a record of the meetings.

during which time competitive uncertainty has given an important coloration to management thinking; (2) continuity of top decision-makers in management during the period of company receivership and competitive uncertainty saved the organization from the added crisis of a change in management; (3) in spite of its size the corporation has a remarkably foreshortened management structure resulting in a top management with detailed knowledge of, and intimate contact with both big and little industrial relations problems; (4) the production-oriented outlook of the company policy-makers has led them to view their industrial relations as an adjunct of production, not separate from it. The result has been a problem approach to collective bargaining, which we will spell out in detail below.

Financial and Competitive Uncertainty

When Mr. Hoffman, president, and Mr. Vance, chairman of the board, took over as receivers of the corporation, they had several alternative choices as to labor policy. To them only one policy made sense—a policy which would foster harmonious relationships between the management and the working force. In the words of Mr. Hoffman:

> An independent company like Studebaker, to survive and grow in the highly competitive automotive industry, must offer motor cars and trucks superior or at least equal to those offered by the larger companies. To meet that goal, full advantage had to be taken of all intangibles entering into value—and particularly those which did not cost us money. Morale and good will of the working force were two such intangibles.

From 1924 on, Studebaker was in a financial decline. The year 1923 set a record in terms of gross sales (exceeded only in war production during World War II).[3]

---

[3] A *Light Six Model,* introduced in 1921, proved successful in invading the light car low-price field. It contributed substantially to the sales volume which reached a record 1923 peak.

The prospect of a continued upward sales trend made Erskine, then president of Studebaker, "bullish." Studebaker, in his opinion, was destined to continue as one of the blue chip securities on the stock market. A high, stable dividend rate would insure this. In 1924, 59 per cent of the profits were paid out in dividends. 1926 saw 79 per cent of the net profits going to the stockholders.[4] Eighty-two per cent of the profits in 1927 were paid out in dividends. Only a little more than a million dollars went back into the business in that year, and practically nothing in succeeding years.

The following year, 1928, heralded the period of living off of accumulated reserves. One hundred six per cent of the profits in 1929 went for dividends. In a vain effort to meet the effects of the 1929 crash and support the company's stock market position, declared dividends reached the level of 506 per cent of net profits in 1930. 1931 saw further inroads made into the reserve and working capital of the company with the payment of dividends representing 341 per cent of net profits. In the same year a renewed attempt to build up volume sales was made with the introduction of the *Rockne* in the low-priced field. The car was manufactured at the Detroit plant until 1933 when all manufacturing operations were consolidated at the South Bend works.

The company went into receivership March 18, 1933, with H. S. Vance, who became chairman of the board in 1935, P. G. Hoffman, who became president in 1935, and A. G. Bean, president of the White Motor

---

[4] This was the year that a specially engineered European car was enthusiastically received at the Paris and London automobile shows. The same car, the *Erskine Six,* was introduced to the American market in 1927. A new attempt was made with this car to secure a foothold in the low-price field. In the same year the new *President Eight* added a luxury car to the line of models. Volume sales were not, however, forthcoming in fulfillment of the trend of 1921–23.

Company (then owned by Studebaker), as the court-appointed receivers. Production was continued under the receivership with a yearly operating loss of approximately one and one-half million dollars for 1933, 1934, and 1935. A refinancing program succeeded in raising approximately six and one-half million in capital and the reorganization plan received court approval January 28, 1935.

Thus Studebaker celebrated its eighty-third year in 1935 by skirting the disaster of business failure. On the come-back road since then, the corporation has made a vigorous bid for a larger segment of the automobile market. It was the first company to introduce a postwar styled car early in 1946.

Under the guidance of Vance and Hoffman the working capital of the business was cautiously rebuilt. This was done in spite of a narrow operating profit. Table 1 on the following page gives the essential facts which point to the delicate financial ground over which the company passed in the postdepression period.[5]

For years Studebaker has been faced with a real competitive problem in the automotive industry. In the period of 1935 through 1941 the company produced an average of 2.1 per cent[6] of the passenger and commercial cars manufactured in this country. In order to expand production well beyond the prewar peak of almost 150,000 vehicles per year, a sizable investment was made in

---

[5] Net sales had not in 1946 returned to the 1923 peak of $160,000,000 on civilian production. In the last prewar year, 1941, the corporation recorded net sales of $115,700,000 compared with the low point of $33,838,000 in 1935. The wartime peak was reached in 1944 with net sales of $415,746,000, the increase representing largely the product of the three plants operated for the Air Corps and manufacturing aircraft engines.

[6] The introduction in 1939 of Studebaker's latest entry into the low-priced field—the *Champion,* saw Ford, General Motors and Chrysler control 90 per cent of the automobile business, and practically all business in low-priced cars. Studebaker, Packard and Hudson existed upon a slim 5 per cent wedge of the medium-priced car market. "Studebaker's Light Car," *Fortune,* XIX, No. 4 (April, 1939), 86.

TABLE 1
Operating Profit, Net Income on Sales and Net Income to Surplus, Studebaker Corp., 1935–45*

Year	Operating Profit ($1000's)	Net Income on Sales†	Net Income to Surplus ($1000's)
1935	−1,593‡	−5.84%	−1,976§
1936	3,336	3.17	2,188
1937	1,458	1.15	812
1938	−1,460‡	−4.03	−1,762§
1939	3,922	3.58	2,923
1940	3,163	2.52	2,125
1941	6,582	2.15	2,486
1942	8,455	0.92	2,048
1943	17,711	0.78	2,835
1944	21,484	0.97	4,038
1945	5,059	1.54	3,277

* From *Moody's Industrials* (New York: Moody's Investors' Service, 1936–46).
† As a percentage of net sales.
‡ Operating loss.
§ Debit.

production facilities following the war. Thus, the company was still faced with a "calculated risk" with respect to its production position.

In brief, the corporation has weathered an era of extreme financial insecurity. The postwar period has been one of optimistic planning with relatively sound financial footing. The achievement of the planned-for goal of a larger share of automobile production lies still in the future. In the past, financial difficulties of the business influenced management's labor relations policy. For the future, competition in the sale of automobile vehicles will be the big problem for the corporation. The emphasis will be on maintaining a labor situation which guarantees stability in the present and predicability for the future.

Continuity of Management

A factor important to an understanding of the company labor policy has been the continuity of top executives through the periods of prosperity, decline, and resurrection. They all have service records which predate the first union organization and the advent of collective bargaining in the plant. They have all experienced the pre-union personnel policies of the concern. They have all been active in the development of the union-management relationship, as policy makers or administrators. Thus, there has been a very stable group of top management people who have had long familiarity with their business, their work force, and their industrial relations policies. The same has been true of supervision, made up largely of long-service employees, almost exclusively promoted from the ranks.

Both Hoffman and Vance have long been associated with the company. Both had known the original Studebaker management, and had risen to top positions under the Erskine presidency. In 1925 Hoffman was brought into the organization from Los Angeles where he had established his reputation as the outstanding salesman in the country at the Los Angeles Studebaker agency. He was made vice-president in charge of sales and promoted to the presidency in 1935.

Vance started in the shop at the old E-M-F company and when that company was purchased by Studebaker he moved up in the management hierarchy. In 1926 he came to South Bend from Detroit and became vice-president in charge of production. He moved to the position of chairman of the board when Hoffman became president.

This continuity of management was particularly important in handling unionization of the plant. The union was organized as a federal local of the AFL just three months after the company went into receivership. Receivers alien to the company and unfamiliar with the workers and the community from which they came might well have given quite a different tone to the start and subsequent development of the union-management relationship.

Simplicity of Management Organization

Another important background development of the company labor policy has been the simplicity of the management structure.[7] There have always been relatively short lines of communication and correspondingly greater direct contact with situations by the top operating officials of the company. Furthermore, the industrial relations functions centered almost completely in the hands of the operating or line organization. The industrial relations group has performed largely in a staff capacity to the operating officials (except with regard to the employment office which has constituted a direct responsibility of the industrial relations director).

The simplicity of the management structure on first consideration seems to be a result of the easy communication between the lowest levels and top decision-makers. But much more important has been the fact that the simple management organization has reflected the role of the top company officials. The chairman of the board of directors, the vice-president in charge of production, the general superintendent, the general foreman, and the director of industrial relations all have had intimate, detailed working knowledge of the plant and production operations. None of these officials has had to depend upon a large staff of technically competent subordinates who, under their direction, acted as their eyes, ears, and technical brains in the handling of production and labor relations problems.

---

[7] Discussed here primarily from the standpoint of industrial relations activity. No specific check was made on the management organization in the areas of sales or engineering and development for example. It is believed, however, that the simplicity of organization which has been found in the labor relations function was characteristic of the company as a whole.

The technical know-how possessed directly by the top officials enabled them to see labor relations problems in all their practical ramifications. They have not sat as judges on a problem, seeking a principle to resolve the conflicting claims of their own technical staff and those of the union. For example, it is characteristic that the vice-president in charge of production does not have to depend upon subordinates to tell him about the details of the acetylene welders' jobs on the body assembly line. He knows the job in all its details. He can meet the union and discuss directly the merits of a claimed inequity in rates between these welders and others in the plant, or the merits of a union claim that the job requires more manpower.

The Problem Approach

This simplified management structure has summed up to the fact that top company operating officials have viewed their industrial relations problems as a part of, not distinct from, their production problems. There has been no essential separation between the two in their minds. The logic of production has been the logic of industrial relations. And the solution of production problems has been immediate, forthright, and to the point. It has not depended upon a highly developed and closely integrated set of principles.

These operating men, then, have handled their labor relations on a problem rather than a principle basis.

One of the company officials gave very apt expression to the idea of the problem approach when he said:

> We go along here with everything quiet and peaceful between us and the union when suddenly we have a crisis. Something isn't just right and there is a lot of excitement. Things begin to look as though a crisis is in the making. Then, just before the breaking point seems to be reached, everything gets settled. We go back to an uneventful period again. I sometimes feel as though we are

sitting on a powder keg with a fuze attached that sputters but always gets put out before it ignites the powder.

The essence of this statement is the belief that there has been no foreordained answer to every dispute between union and management. The individual disagreements have been resolved in a crisis atmosphere which lasted only until the problem was settled.

This problem approach has been fortified by the philosophy of the corporation president. He rose to the presidency because he was the leading Studebaker salesman in the country. In conversations with him he gave a twist to the creed that "the customer is always right." He stated, "The best way to lose a sale is to win an argument." When applied to the conduct of industrial relations this doctrine has a fundamental democratic foundation. The management's case in a discussion with the union has been only as good as it was convincing to the union representatives. It became unconvincing exactly in proportion as it has made use of, or implied, coercion.

Studebaker's management policy of always "talking out" every problem with the union has followed directly from this precept. There has been no basic issue in the union-management relationship with an automatic solution. Basically, the management has wanted the union to believe in, and hence actively support, an agreement reached at the bargaining table. The "talking out" of a problem has been the process of exposing to view, and thereby understanding, all the facts relevant to the problem. There has been no a priori assumption that management either had all the pertinent facts or had necessarily reasoned to a proper conclusion on the basis of them. The decision, in so far as it has involved the union at all, was a joint one. The basis of the decision has been the joint examination and "self-selling" of each party on the facts of the case and the adequacy of the conclusions reached from the facts. It should be emphasized that the "talking out" policy of the management, while a "selling" device, has not been designed as a stall to out talk and wear down union resistance to the management ideas, leaving the management the winner in the end.

COMPANY LABOR POLICY

These four background factors give us a key to an understanding of the labor policy of the Studebaker Corporation. This policy has faced the reality of the economic position of the corporation. It has been made by men who have been connected with the company for a long period of time, knowing intimately the company, the community, the workers, and the past company practices. It has confronted labor problems as necessary adjuncts of production problems, to be handled in essentially the same way. The policy may be summed up in the broad sociological concept that groups work together best when the resolution of problems has not been solely on the basis of a balance of power, but has also included collaboration for mutual benefit. The salesman president and the production minded chairman of the board and vice-president have come to the same conclusions, but by different means.

In the broadest sense the corporation labor policy has always been to concentrate its approach to collective bargaining on the solution of problems. Principles have been important only if they work in real situations. The company could ill afford to have taken a do-or-die stand in an actual situation just as a matter of eternal principle.[8] Through experience, workable substitutes have been forged which satisfy both the management and the union.

---

[8] Compare, for example, with the 110 day strike at GM and the basis of it as set forth in Chapter II.

Following the Pattern

The company is in business to make a profit. Its planning has always been based upon that expectation. Labor costs are controlled, in part, by following the Detroit automotive pattern hammered out by the "Big Three" with the UAW. On all union-management problems which involve money the company has used as its first yardstick the industry pattern as reflected by Detroit practices, particularly at General Motors. The company has never been the leader on such matters. It has always conformed to the industry pattern. This has been recognized by both sides and has become a conscious part of the union-management relationship. Thus, the first principle of the company labor policy has been to maintain its pattern-following position with respect to money matters in relations with the union.

A Price on Concessions

Another guiding principle of the management policy has been that each concession to the union must have some compensating value for the company. There has to be something in it for the company; the company has to be "self-sold" on its advantage in the proposed "deal."

It is at this point that the company has deviated from a fairly common managerial pattern. The management has taken a broad, long-range view of what it gets out of a particular agreement with the union. And most important, it has given consideration to intangibles that cannot be precisely measured. There has been no strict accounting procedure of keeping mental balance sheets in imaginary books. Such a factor as morale may carry equal importance with a ten cent saving in direct labor cost of a piston assembly. This goes back to the knowledge and "sense of feel" the management has had about the work situation.

Security for the Union

The third principle of the company labor policy has been the recognition that a stable union organization is important to stability in the union-management relationship. The company executives have taken great pains to recognize the offices, positions and status of union officials. There has never been any manifest management attempt to compete with the union for worker loyalty.

Top management at Studebaker has considered security for the union an important prerequisite for responsible unionism. Management has recognized that a strong and stable union establishes itself with difficulty if it is told to go out and continually organize in order to maintain membership. Accordingly, Studebaker management has encouraged security for the union by joining with it in sponsoring employee activities or leaving certain fields of employee activities entirely to the union. The most obvious illustration of management's concern with stability of the union occurred during the war. Each new employee received a company letter pointing out the importance of the union in worker-company relations. As a consequence the union was unusually stable during a period of considerable expansion in the work force. Union membership was virtually 100 per cent among the new workers.

The company executives, on the other hand, have been strongly opposed to a contract clause requiring compulsory union membership. They have considered it inconsistent with the idea of freedom for the individual. The management has further felt that its bargaining position has been safeguarded if its workers were not automatically tied to the union. This second consideration has been probably only of intangible value since the union has had all the strength, and even more, that it would have had under a contract guarantee of membership.

Within the structure of management equal attention has been directed by the top executives to building and maintaining a stable executive and supervisory group. The result has been that union and company face each other as strong and stable organizations.

The four background factors (competitive uncertainty, continuity of management, simplicity of management structure, and a problem approach to collective bargaining) have reached expression in a three-part labor policy of the corporation. The company first of all has followed the industry pattern on money matters involved in collective bargaining. Secondly, the company has put a price on every concession to the union. Finally, the company policy makers have recognized that a prerequisite of a stable union-management relationship, capable of maintaining its stability in a general economic atmosphere of rapid change and uncertainty, has depended upon organizational soundness on both sides of the bargaining table.

How does this approach to collective bargaining work out in actual practice? Before we can answer that question it is necessary to examine the union and its policies. Then we can see where management and union policies mesh and where they clash.

THE UNION AND ITS MEMBERS

Local 5, UAW-CIO had, in 1947, what amounted to a practical union shop in the Studebaker plant. At the same time, and unlike some unions which have 100 per cent membership of the bargaining unit, this union's membership body has played a major role in determination of union policy. An officer of this local union has importance and prestige as a representative of the membership. His prestige has not arisen from his power to shape the policies of the union apart from membership desires.

Let us look at some of the broad facts characterizing the work force in the plant and the community from which the workers come. From these facts we can gain an understanding of the character of this union.

A Stable Community Background

The population of South Bend and St. Joseph County, Indiana,[9] has always been stable and rooted to the community. This is in sharp contrast to Detroit. Detroit has a heterogeneous population, a large portion of which has recently taken up residence there. The Detroit community ties are less strong and the differences between population groups outweigh the similarities which serve as the bond of community cohesion.

Here are some of the facts on the relative stability of the population. Little change occurred in the total population of the South Bend area between 1930 and 1940. The city showed a 2.5 per cent decrease in population while the county increased in total population by 1.1 per cent. Many of the workers in the community live in single family dwellings. Fifty-five per cent of all dwelling units in the county were owner occupied in 1940, 11 per cent higher than the national average of home ownership. In 1940, 88.1 per cent of the population of the county was native white, 9.6 per cent foreign-born white. In the 1936 Census of Religious Bodies, of all those in South Bend who indicated their religious affiliation, 55 per cent were members of the Roman Catholic Church.

---

[9] Two years before the Studebaker wagon works was established there in 1852, the population of South Bend, Indiana, totalled 1,652. By 1940 the city numbered a little over 100,000 residents. St. Joseph County, in which South Bend is located and from which the work force of Studebaker is drawn, had a corresponding population of 161,000 in 1940.

The area is largely urban in character. The 1940 census showed that four out of every five county inhabitants lived in areas classified as urban. Furthermore, the area is largely industrial. In 1940, 80 per cent of the 21,000 wage earners in the county were employed in industry in South Bend.

Most important of all in understanding the way the workers have looked at their employment opportunities in the community has been the fact that 55 per cent of the industrial wage earners worked in motor vehicle and parts plants. Studebaker has been by far the largest single employer in the area. With employment of about 12,000 (1946) it was estimated that the corporation employed approximately half of the industrial workers in the area. Thus, the economic well-being of the area has been largely tied to the prosperity and continued existence of the Studebaker Corporation.

Everyone in the plant and in the community has been mindful of the fact that Studebaker has been the underdog in competition with the "Big Three" of the automotive industry. The exact statistics may not be known but the understanding has been clear that Studebaker was small in the industry, though all-important in the community.

Some insight into the close ties between company and community can be secured by examining certain of the findings of a general public opinion poll conducted in October, 1945 at the South Bend community. This poll, supervised by one of the professional organizations in this field, covered a cross-section of the citizens of South Bend and Mishawaka. One part of the survey dealt with the industrial life of the community. Some of the responses to certain questions revealed the position of Studebaker as a place to work.

The community[10] thought that Studebaker was the best place to work. The company was picked as the best by 42 per cent of the people—the highest of any company. Not only was Studebaker the favorite generally in the community but also ranked first among the workers employed in other South Bend plants. When asked further questions to answer why a particular plant stood high in the community, the general responses indicated that: (1) Studebaker of all the companies has taken the most interest in the welfare of its workers (36 per cent of the respondents); (2) the company has cooperated best with the union of all the companies (said 59 per cent of those replying); (3) the company paid the highest wages (according to almost 7 out of 10 of those surveyed). On each of these three factors Studebaker topped all the other companies. A further question as to which company did most for the community showed Studebaker leading the rest as the choice of 38 per cent of the people interviewed.

Opinion polls of this sort are, perhaps, more valuable in providing clues to people's attitudes than they are in giving a definitive picture of how people really feel. Perhaps a better test of the regard with which Studebaker has been held by the community has been the ease with which the company has always been able to recruit additional workers as needed. Even during the period of the most critical labor shortage during the war, Studebaker had relatively little trouble expanding its work force. This was more remarkable in view of the competition of a very large ordnance plant within easy commuting distance of the South Bend area. The union president reported in 1947 that if and when a night shift were added at the

---

[10] In reporting on the community attitude towards Studebaker, we have excluded from the sample all those who were Studebaker employees.

plant, there were many workers employed by other firms who would immediately want to go to work at Studebaker. We can conclude that whether or not the opinion poll accurately reflected the reasons people think Studebaker a good place to work, the evidence nevertheless was strong that many of the residents of the South Bend area look forward to an opportunity to work in the plant.

To what extent has the work force at Studebaker been a cross-section of the community population? Some idea can be secured by comparing the age distribution of the Studebaker workers with that of the area from which they come. The figures are given in Table 2.

TABLE 2

AGE OF MALE WORKERS AT STUDEBAKER CORPORATION AND MALES IN ST. JOSEPH COUNTY, INDIANA, 1940*

Age Group	Per Cent of Males	
	Studebaker	St. Joseph Co.
20–24	2.2%	12.6%
25–29	8.5	12.4
30–34	13.3	12.1
35–39	17.3	12.0
40–44	16.2	11.2
45–49	15.2	9.9
50 and over	27.2	29.8
Total	100.0%	100.0%

* From the records of the company for Studebaker workers; from the 1940 census for St. Joseph County.

It is evident from the table that the corporation has employed a cross-section of the male population with emphasis on the middle and older age groups. When this picture is contrasted with the age distribution for automobile industry workers in general, as is done in Table 3, it is clear that Studebaker has tailored its work force to the community and not the practice of the industry. For example, the industry employed only 27.6 per cent of its total male workers among the group 45 years of age and over, while at Studebaker these employees represented 42.4 per cent of the work force.

TABLE 3

Age of Male Workers at Studebaker Corporation and Workers Employed in the Automobile and Equipment Industry, 1940*

Age Group	Per Cent of Males	
	Studebaker	Auto Industry
Under 20	0.1%	1.5%
20–24	2.2	11.0
25–34	21.8	31.6
35–44	33.5	28.3
45–54	27.8	19.5
55 and over	14.6	8.1
Total	100.0%	100.0%

* From the records of the company for Studebaker workers; from the 1940 census for the automobile industry.

Studebaker Workers

Let us now turn our attention to the Studebaker workers. How closely have they been really identified with the company? For one thing, the length of service figures give us some idea of how long they have been employed with the company. The record is unusual for a mass production industry which in the very recent past had the reputation for discharging its older workers as incapable of maintaining the required speed of production. Table 4 on the following page shows that there is a large number of present employees whose working life has been long identified with the corporation. The work force at Studebaker has not been a "pick up team." It has played together on the home lot for a long time.[11]

[11] The corporation has for a long time featured in its national advertising the "father-son" aspect of its work force. There has been considerable employment of family members in the plant as a matter of conscious selection policy on the part of the company. This, of course, has added still another bond which has tended to knit the work force into a more closely related unit.

TABLE 4

LENGTH OF SERVICE OF STUDEBAKER EMPLOYEES, 1935 AND 1946*

Number of Years of Service	Percentage of Employees in—	
	March, 1935	November, 1946
Under 5 years	21.4%	23.5%
5–9	31.6	32.4
10–14	34.9	12.3
15–19	8.4	7.6
20 and over	3.7	24.2
Total	100.0%	100.0%

* From company personnel records.

These workers have been strongly identified with the company as a place to work. The opinion poll mentioned above indicated that 87 per cent of the sample of workers employed at Studebaker felt that the company was the best place in town to work. A little over seven out of every ten of them thought this management the most interested in the welfare of the employees of all the managements in town. Almost all agreed (93 per cent said so) that the company paid the highest wages, and cooperated best with the union (91 per cent). Three out of every five thought that the company had done most of all companies for the community.

Self-conscious Union Membership

Local 5, UAW-CIO, the Studebaker union, was originally chartered by the AFL as a federal labor union, July 21, 1933. (It will be remembered that the company was in receivership at that time.) In October, 1935 the membership voted to affiliate with the CIO. It was not until May 21, 1937, four years after the union was organized, that a written agreement was signed with the company. In those four years bargaining was carried forward on the basis of a company statement of policy.

Membership of this local has been very much aware of its role in controlling the union officials. This is all summed up in one phrase: "the body." There has been constant reference in the meetings between management and union officials to "the body" and to "the boys"—meaning the membership. Almost every issue gets discussed in the light of what "the body" wanted or what it would do. In a very real sense the union officials have been the intermediaries between union members and management.

It has not been unusual for a union divisional representative (general steward) to come into a grievance situation in the shop and determine the union position in arguing the case with management by taking a vote on the spot of the desires of the members involved. It has been the general practice for all matters to be submitted to the weekly meeting of "the body" for a decision by vote.

The members of this local union have always felt that they collectively control the union. For example, in 1946, when certain intraplant wage inequities were being straightened out, the union president refused to give the company any promise that future demands would not be brought up on inequities. The president's position was that "the body" would never go along with an artificial freeze on future action. It would be insincere of him even to attempt to make such a commitment for the membership when it was "the body" which would raise the question of new inequities if it saw fit.

The union officials have emphasized over and over again to management that they act on a mandate from the membership, with no power to commit the union to a policy without membership consent. If we look back at the factors which characterize the stability of this work force, the strong ties which the workers have with the community, and the long time association with each other as fellow workers, it is not at all strange that the union has always been composed of members who identify themselves with it to a greater extent than is found among the membership of many local unions.

Further indication of the self-consciousness of union membership has been the pressure within the shop to have all workers join the union. Union membership has become one of the necessary badges of a fellow worker. There has really been no need for a union shop clause in the contract. The individual union members and officials have always been vigilant in that regard. During the war the company supported union membership in order to take care of the problem of people not part of the regular work force. Such support was discontinued after the war and has certainly no longer been necessary.

Self-sufficient Local

The "grass roots" aspect of this local union has perhaps been most evident in its relations with the International Union. It has been the general practice within the International to have central administration officials, regional directors and their staffs, participate in contract negotiations and the settlement of grievances at the higher levels of the grievance procedure. No International representative has ever been called in to assist the Studebaker local in dealing with management. Local 5 has been in no sense a "hot house" growth which needs constant ministrations from the parent organization.

On the other hand, it is false to conclude that the International Union is of minor importance to the local. Remember the Studebaker collective bargaining has operated on the principle of pattern-following. Local 5 gets the general tone of its demands from its parent organization. A good share of the bargaining power of this local union has derived from the implicit strength of the International Union. Furthermore the International has always been the source of information on details of the pattern established at the "Big Three." Without the services of the International, the local would have had a much more difficult job in securing the facts in support of its bargaining position. In the kind of collective bargaining found at Studebaker, this research and information service has been of prime importance to Local 5.

Inside the Union

The activities of the union have centered at the union hall, a large building situated close to the plant. Here the weekly meetings of the union are held. Every Friday night the membership meets to transact the business of the union. At routine meetings two to four hundred members, on the average, are present. Much larger turnouts have attended meetings at which important matters were discussed.

This weekly meeting feature has been important in the chain of communication of the union. It has afforded an opportunity for the membership to keep abreast of the activities of the officers in general matters. At the same time, these frequent meetings have kept top officers of the union in close contact with the desires of the membership. Other links in the communication chain include frequent stewards meetings. In addition, the stewards meet with their particular constituents on local departmental problems.

One of the results of these regular and frequent meetings of officials and members has been to keep "the body" up to date on new policy and management decisions in grievance cases. Often the union's communication to the rank and file has been more rapid than that of management to its supervisors. This is a problem which management has not yet satisfactorily solved. The result has sometimes been one of having the workers informed earlier than their supervisors of changes in the shop.

While this situation tends to devalue the supervisor's position, it has had positive value in cementing union solidarity. When the union member can get his first knowledge of a change affecting the shop from his own people, and talk out the reasons for such change, the change itself comes about without the opprobrium of management dictate. It isn't the foreman who says so because his superiors have made a decision; it is the union itself which presents the case as one in which the union has played an active role in making the decision. This process has served to take out of the union-management relationship much of the feeling that decisions affecting the work force are made on a "that's it—take it or leave it" basis.

The holding of an elective office in Local 5 has always carried with it a very considerable amount of prestige. The prestige has been based upon the sense of importance which attaches to being the spokesman for a powerful group. It has not been the prestige which derives from a position of power to dictate the activities of followers. The difference is crucial. In the first case the organization retains many aspects of control over its own policy. In the second case the membership is solidified on the basis of fear of the leader's power.

The evidence supporting this conclusion is clear. No union president has held that office more than two years. From 1936 to 1946 there have been seven different presidents, four of them having been re-elected for one additional term.[12] The bargaining committee, composed of

---

[12] George C. Hupp, a veteran of seventeen years' service with the company, was in 1947 serving his second term as president of Local 5. William L. Gregory, employed at Studebaker for twenty-two years, was re-elected vice-president for a second term in 1947. Both of these officials, aggressive leaders of the union, have reflected, from their long years of experience at Studebaker, the thinking and reactions of the union members.

the divisional representatives and the president and vice-president, has changed with each yearly election, but with hold-overs in each year. The shop stewards have an average length of service of three to four years.

There have been factions within this local, to be expected in any organization based upon a representative form of government. These factions, however, do not conform to the left-right split found so widely throughout the UAW. Competition for office has been on an "ins vs. outs" basis. There has been no wholesale housecleaning of opponents with the advent of each new administration. This does not mean, of course, that the political rivalry has been less keen. Each incumbent administration has always had to face the rivalry of its defeated opponents.

Two important controls insure that no administration can gain control with only minority support. In the elections for union offices, published electioneering effort has been limited to the printing of a special union bulletin carrying photographs of the candidates and their qualifications. No other material has been permitted. At the same time, to insure wide participation in the election of top union officials, a fine has been imposed on those members who fail to vote for the offices of president, vice-president, and other general officials.

Mere formal membership in the union is, of course, an insufficient base for tieing the membership together. Supplementing the primary economic role which the union plays for its membership have been the non-collective bargaining union functions. A library of over 3,000 books has been maintained at the union headquarters with a full time librarian in charge. Lectures and discussion groups have been provided as additional educational activities. A cooperative grocery store has been aggressively supported by the union. The camera club has a number of active participants. With the housing crisis, the union established a cooperative housing project. On 157 acres of land it proposes to build 500 to 1,000 homes costing approximately $5,500 each on a cooperative basis, compared with an estimated $9,000 in the private market. This housing project will be open to other union members in the South Bend area.

The community has been very much aware of the Studebaker local as an organized force in community life. For example, the union makes annual awards to the outstanding vocational student in each of the five high schools in South Bend and Mishawaka. This local organized and actively supported the Rural-Urban council which has been designed as a forum to bring farmers and factory workers together to discuss mutual problems. The union has individual members, who represent either the local union or the local labor movement on such community agencies as the council of social agencies. Some of the individual union members have been active in politics as spokesmen for the labor bloc and several have held local or state elective offices.

In short, the union has stood as a center for a number of nonworking activities of its members. The community has recognized this large organized force within the body politic, and by such acceptance has tended to legitimize and strengthen the ties of the members to the organization.

To summarize, the union has been accepted by the membership as a responsive, dynamic part of the workaday world. In the community at large the union has an established part in the social fabric of the town. As a result the union has had "grass root" characteristics attuned to the outlook of its members and the community in which they live.

BROAD UNION POLICY

This brings us to a consideration of the larger aspects of union policy. What, after all, are the broad goals which constitute the reasons for the existence of a labor organization in the Studebaker Corporation? There are four points in the union program which give us the key to an understanding of the union side of the labor-management relationship.

Economic Uncertainty

Economic uncertainty is a matter of recent memory to the Studebaker work force. Almost one third of the workers in the plant in 1947 went through the depression and receivership as Studebaker employees.[13] They remember the loss of work and the humanitarian but not totally adequate measures the company took to relieve some of the hardships of unemployment.[14] To them company survival was an essential. But some balance had to be struck between company earnings and worker income. From the worker's point of view the sacrifice was shared with the expectation of a similar sharing of gains. In short, out of the general feeling of insecurity arose a pointed awareness of the corporation's "ability to pay."

We have already seen that the company went through a period of crisis struggling for its very survival. The workers and the community had front row seats in observing the struggle; the difficulties were never a closely held management secret. With the management, of necessity, focusing on cost reduction and stabilization, the employees were made acutely aware of possible impinge-

---

[13] Cf. Table 4, p. 122.

[14] During the depths of the depression the management set up a canning project within the plant, providing produce from the local farms. Studebaker employees were able to produce canned foods to supplement direct purchases from retail stores, and thus stretch their meager resources.

ment on their own economic status. Regardless of the broad social outlook of the management in wishing to preserve a community enterprise giving a livelihood to many thousands of employees, the latent suspicion of workers was always present that jobs would be preserved, but at the expense of wages and income. To them management was after all first accountable to the stockholders. After that interest was satisfied with the health of the enterprise, only then could the welfare of the workers be given primary attention.

It is probable that this company would not have been organized so early after the start of the organizing drive on mass production industries but for the general growth of unionism during the middle thirties. However, once union organization became general and sanctioned by public policy, the workers in this plant found in unionism a significant way to protect themselves against possible exploitation to save the company's existence during the period of receivership.

Thus, the union has always been vitally interested in the company's "ability to pay." It has been a cardinal purpose of the union to insure that the company has in fact come close to the limits of its ability to pay. But what sets the limits? Where could the company feel that it had a proper right to say "that is all"? Must it always "look at the books" and come up with an accounting answer to this question? The answer is found in "following the pattern."

Following the Pattern

The union has come to accept as right and proper the Detroit wage pattern (usually set by General Motors). When this policy was accepted by the company in 1938 it represented an important concession to the union at a time when the company was certainly not out of financial danger. Studebaker workers could not expect more than other auto workers in terms of pay and "fringe" income. But if they could hope to at least equal the Detroit standards they would be in a comparatively sound position. Thus, the Detroit yardstick on financial matters made sense to the workers.[15]

Job Control

There have always been many aspects of the workaday life which are of vital significance to the workers and which extend beyond the pay envelope. We have noted above, for example, the unusually large proportion of Studebaker workers who have twenty or more years service with the company. To such workers the matter of seniority has become a matter of deep concern. But in addition to the seniority question has been the one of finding in the plant a sufficient number of jobs on which older and slower men can be placed. These are simply two out of countless problems that fall within the scope of "working conditions." To the union and its membership, control, through the device of joint negotiation with the company, has always been a vital necessity in the area of job conditions.

Another aspect of the control objectives of the union has to do with the policing of its own members. Once union control over job conditions becomes stabilized, means must be devised to prevent upsetting the applecart. For example, under the incentive system, two groups having the same job classification, and hence the same base rate, cannot show consistent and widely differing take-home pay without trouble resulting. The union has

---

[15] We will see later that the wages have actually been higher at Studebaker than the industry averages. This has been due to the incentive system at Studebaker. The base rates under this incentive system have been equated with the Detroit standards.

found itself policing or controlling the development of such possible divergencies in the interests of holding down group or individual rivalries among its members.

Consciousness of Status

The union's fourth objective has been the development and continuation of its relative equality with the company in bargaining power. There has been an all pervading consciousness of the power status of the union in relation to management. The best summary of this feeling was contained in a statement made by one of the union officials at a bargaining meeting. The company appeared to be making a "take it or leave it offer." The union president indignantly stated:

> Are you saying, "There it is, period"? If you are, I want you to know we are not going to sit still for anything like that. We have worked long and hard to discuss problems with management and work them out. We want to keep doing that. But if you want to go back to this "Take it or else . . ." basis, we can play ball like that too, don't forget that.

This same consciousness of status and power has been expressed again in one of the standing jokes among the union officialdom. With mock seriousness a steward will say, "Guess we'll have to pull that department down until we can get this thing settled," or, "The boys won't sit still any longer on that one." These pat phrases have been used within the union ranks as a mark of the latent militancy of leaders and members. Actual use of economic power has been resorted to a sufficient number of times through short work stoppages and slowdowns to convince everyone concerned that direct action was still part of the arsenal of this union's weapons.

Company and Union Policy

There has always been pride on both sides of the bargaining table in the unusually fine record of industrial peace in the company. But no one on either side has been lulled into a feeling of false security believing that, come what may, the workers would never strike. The union and management have always believed that their way of settling differences was a good one. Neither side has ever seriously thought that peaceful settlement of issues has vitiated "the body's" faith in direct action, given the proper circumstances.

Summary

In summary it can be stated that two factors have been common to the company and union policies: (1) the competitive uncertainty of the company which gave a strong, but not identical, impetus to union and management in the development of a particular pattern of collective bargaining and (2) the agreement to let Detroit set the money standards to which Studebaker has adjusted the South Bend pay envelope. The union operating in an atmosphere of union security, actively fostered by the company, has focused a large share of its attention on securing control of job conditions through collective bargaining. There has been no motive of "taking over management" involved in this. Job control has been viewed as a necessary step in the protection of the workers against the risks of industry. By engaging in the direction of the work force as an active party in a number of significant aspects the union has come to have a greater respect for the conditions surrounding the workday at Studebaker. After all, the union has become directly involved in making and administering work rules. Finally, the union has guarded jealously its power status in the collective bargaining relationship by controlling possible sources of division within its own ranks. Much of the character of the collective bargaining atmosphere has been derived from the stable balance of power existing between union and company.

CHAPTER V

Collective Bargaining between Studebaker and Local 5, UAW-CIO

IT is possible to make a very accurate guess from what we now know of the management and union motivations and policies at Studebaker that the scope of collective bargaining has been almost unlimited. Reading the union contract gives no indication of the limits containing union demands. Theoretically nothing is outside the reach of the union. Practically, however, the union "knows its place" and there has been little controversy with management on the latter's function to manage.

The "problem" has always been the unit of action for both sides. The guiding principles in the solution of these problems have already been set forth in the analysis of company and union policies. The problem approach is first of all illustrated in the contract itself. The union agreement is open-ended, renewable yearly by mutual consent. It can be revised or amended at any time. The very terms of the contract are not even frozen for a fixed period of time. Yet in spite of this the agreement has a continuing identity with its first formulation in 1937.

The 1946 union contract, for example, still carried the statement, "This agreement, entered into this 21st day of May, 1937 . . . ." The significance of this phrase in the contract lies in the fact that both sides have felt that the basic document signed in 1937 was still good enough to govern their relationship in 1946. In a real sense the union contract has been a "living constitution" establishing the rights and obligations of each side towards the other.

MANAGEMENT PREROGATIVES AND UNION JOB CONTROL

The Studebaker contract has not contained a management prerogative clause. In the November, 1944 contract negotiations such a clause was the major proposal of the company. It was pointed out by the management that the proposed clause was identical with those appearing in other contracts of the International Union. From the company standpoint the purpose of the clause was to make sure that the union clearly understood that the management would have to make a whole series of critical unilateral decisions, come reconversion to peacetime production. In the words of President Hoffman at the bargaining meeting:

> Whether or not such a clause is written into the contract is not itself important. But we want everyone around this table to understand what a management is for. If you thoroughly understand that we are satisfied.

The union gave full assent to the statement of management functions as outlined by the company executives. It was, after all, what the International had accepted in contracts with other companies. The objection to writing it into the contract was two-fold. Union officials pointed out that with possible reductions in force in the offing, anticipating probable effects of reconversion adjustments, such a clause would create suspicion that management wanted to get tough. More important, the union contended that such a clause would destroy the mutual understanding which existed in the handling of grievances and in the way in which the union-management relationship had been built up. Union officers reported that "the body" had strong feelings on this subject. In fact, in one meeting of a night force group the clause was rejected by a vote of 191 to 7. In a later combined meeting of the day and night shifts the clause was unanimously rejected.

Such a clause has not been written into the contract. The union officials have stated that they will be adamant for a union shop clause if management insists on the prerogatives clause. The union has not needed a formal union shop since membership has been 100 per cent of the eligible work force. In the same sense, management has not needed its clause since no one in the local union has disputed management's functions. The union has feared that such a clause would be the forerunner of formalism in the union-management relationship. The union shop demand has simply been the union's way of matching possible company legalism.

What has the union got to lose by fixed and formal collective bargaining? Job control—within the limits of freedom of action by management or union in the local plant situation—is the union's stake. This becomes more evident in the detailed discussion which follows. Suffice to point out here that it would be almost impossible to reduce to a written, formal document the "union prerogatives." It would take a volume to record all the details.

THE WAGE ISSUE

Before going into the details of the complete union-management relationship it is necessary to ask one crucial question. Is the cooperation between union and management a way of "buying off" the union on wages? If we look at it from the standpoint of the worker's take-home the answer is a clear "no." The Studebaker worker's take-home has been substantially above the industry average. How much is indicated in Table 5.

What has accounted for the ability of a company, not the competitive leader in its field, to pay wages in excess

TABLE 5

Average Hourly Earnings—Studebaker Corporation and the Automobile and Parts Industry*

Period	Average Hourly Earnings† Studebaker	Auto and Parts Industry
1941		
1st Half	105.8¢	99.8¢
2nd Half	114.3	108.6
1942		
1st Half	122.6	115.6
2nd Half	123.9	118.2
1943		
1st Half	138.0	122.2
2nd Half	147.8	124.6
1944		
1st Half	160.9	126.3
2nd Half	163.9	127.8
1945		
1st Half	167.3	128.2
2nd Half	149.3	123.0
1946		
1st Half	147.0	128.0
2nd Half	159.2	137.1

* From the U.S. Dept. of Commerce *Survey of Current Business* for the Automobile and Parts Industry; from the records of the company for Studebaker.
† The automobile industry figures are an average of the monthly figures for each period. The Studebaker figures include only employees at the parent plant. Excluded from the Studebaker figures are the earnings of its wartime employees in three aircraft engine and parts plants where the average hourly earnings were even higher than in the parent plant.

of the industry average? The answer can be found in a long established incentive wage payment system. Under the Studebaker plan the company has been able to stabilize its unit labor cost and share directly with its workers increased production.

It has always been the present management's philosophy that all that's due to the workers in money should appear in today's pay envelope. There has been a strong management desire to avoid buying off today's pay increase with the promise of a lump sum (a bonus, for example) at some one time in the year. President Hoffman expressed this pointedly in a bargaining meeting with the union which requested a Christmas bonus under the WLB edict automatically approving such bonuses if they did not exceed twenty-five dollars.

> .... but our philosophy has always been this—and we thought we were right in it, that you want us to pack in the weekly pay envelope every dime we can. You don't want the turkeys, you don't want roses on Mother's Day, you don't want a Christmas bonus—but you want every bit of pay you can get in your pay envelope. That has always seemed to us to be the basis of a sound relationship. .... Now I think that is basically sound policy. It's completely divorced from the old paternalistic attitude that used to prevail in industry—to keep wages down and give you a Christmas bonus, and make you feel happy about it.

The bonus was not granted.

Where then does the matter of "Detroit wage pattern" fit into the picture? The issue centers around wage rates. It has been the joint agreement of company and union that Detroit has set the wage pattern in terms of rates. This then has become the base from which the incentive earnings of Studebaker workers have been calculated. For example, the point was made quite clear in the following exchange between the company vice-president and the union president during a bargaining meeting in 1945. The company vice-president said: "I don't think it was the intent to push Studebaker's rates beyond General Motors'. I don't think that has been the intent—is that right?" The union president replied, "That's right."

The company and union policy of following the Detroit pattern has been of long standing. When the problem of postwar wage increases was raised a decision had to be made by the company without a pattern to follow. Effective August 20, 1945, the corporation granted a twelve cent general wage increase to be applied against the pattern, once established. The union had asked twenty-five cents but accepted this settlement as a down payment. After the 1945–46 GM strike was settled a further adjustment to the full eighteen and one-half cents was made at Studebaker.[1]

The incentive wage system gave rise to a considerable spread between the pay for hourly and incentive workers. This differential in earnings became even more important in 1946 when the cost of living rise pinched workers no longer receiving extensive premium pay for overtime work. Both the union and company recognized it as a problem. An answer finally worked out was to put indirect labor on incentive also, with incentive pay tied to the output of productive workers served. The company proposed a plan whereby the number of indirect workers was reduced so that those savings could be applied on the incentive for the remaining indirect labor force.

Two things stood out in this program: (1) It was introduced at a time when employment was expanding. The displaced workers were reabsorbed in other jobs in the plant; none became unemployed. (2) The company preferred this plan to a straight raise in the hourly rates of indirect labor. Thus, the incentive was paid on the same base hourly rates as existed before the plan. As stated by one of the company officials:

> The differentials between direct labor on incentives and indirect labor on hourly rates has become too great. The union is pressuring us on this. Rather than make a change in the base rates of hourly workers, we have gone to an incentive plan for indirect labor. The union is going for the plan and we are now ironing out the details. There is no disagreement on the principle.

The plan was started in October, 1946, and in the first three weeks of its operation resulted in the payment of about a 12 per cent incentive for indirect labor. Union leaders and membership were encouraged about the results. The plan dealt directly with one of the great

---

[1] One of the most interesting aspects of this final settlement had to do with adjustment of inequities. This is discussed later under the heading "The Iniquitous Inequity Adjustments."

sources of worker dissatisfaction in the plant. Both sides secured something out of it; the union by securing wage increases, the company by reducing the size of the indirect labor force.

The incentive plan for indirect labor continued in effect until the middle of December. At that time the plan was discontinued and indirect labor was given a flat 15 per cent increase over base rates. The principal reason for discontinuing the program was the fact that production fluctuated so widely between departments as to create wide weekly changes in the pay for non-production workers. Thus, sweepers in the same job classification, but working in different departments to whose output their incentive bonus was tied, might have as much as ten cents an hour differential in their hourly pay. This is still another example of the way in which bargaining on problems develops. The non-direct labor incentive plan looked good on paper but in actual operation was found to be unsuited in its existing form to the plant conditions at Studebaker. Finally the plan was junked. It was agreed that the problem was to receive further study with the objective of devising another incentive plan at a future date.

It seems clear from the above evidence that the corporation has not bought lower wage rates with its cooperative attitude towards the union. The corporation has secured relatively stabilized labor costs. How much, on the other hand, has the favorable take-home pay of the Studebaker workers put them in a frame of mind to reciprocate the company's cooperativeness? When they judge themselves by the community pay envelopes (93 per cent in the opinion survey mentioned previously said they were paid best) or the industry pay envelopes they obviously have "a good deal." It would be foolish to underrate this favorable take-home pay factor as a base for constructive industrial relations.

It would give us only a very incomplete picture, however, to stop at this point and assume that adequate pay has been the sufficient condition of union-management peace and stable labor relations. All that follows points to other and equally important bases for such union-management relations.

THE NATURE OF THE BARGAINING PROCESS

The "problem" approach to collective bargaining which has always characterized the Studebaker union-management relationship can be spelled out in more detail. In the broadest sense the company has set the objectives for production and sales and maintained direct control over financial affairs, production methods and research. The company has determined without reference to the union the over-all strategy of the business and its place in the economy as a whole. At those points where the grand strategy of the company has been reduced to specific tactical operations involving the work force in some way, the union has entered the picture as a participant in specific decisions. In short, to paraphrase military parlance, the company has had firmly in its grasp the general staff function of determining the over-all strategy of business operations. The union has worked within the framework of company-determined strategy but at many points has become involved in tactical planning to carry it out.

It is characteristic that the management people have seldom used the phrases "The company proposes . . . ." or "The company position is . . . ." The personal "we" or "I" has usually been substituted. The company, in so far as it enters into the union-management relationship, generally has meant the board of directors of the company. On a number of occasions President Hoffman has placed himself in the position of go-between for the union and the board of directors. He has put the situation in the following fashion:

> You and I have made an agreement here which you finally sold me on. I took it to the board and after much opposition finally got them to see the thing the way we worked it out. Now they are holding me responsible for getting the results which we both think will come out of this. It certainly puts me out on a limb and I am depending upon you fellows (union) not to let me down. If this plan fails I will have a much harder time with the board the next time.

In precisely the same fashion the union officials have placed themselves in the position of go-between for the company and "the body." The union officials, of course, speak as the voice of "the body." But they also speak to the membership as the primary channel of communication from the company. It is not merely that they report to the membership. There has been a tendency to recapitulate the negotiations and present some of the arguments on both sides that were the basis of the ultimate joint solution to the problem.

In a sense the "bargaining of representatives" has put the bargaining process in a fish bowl.[2] Both sets of negotiators are being watched by their respective constituents. While both sides have had certain mandates which set limits on the extent to which they could compromise, within the area of their discretion they have been more inclined to argue toward a give and take solution than to take a fixed position and say "that or else . . . ." The fish bowl atmosphere has made any agreement a personal one in which each negotiator was committed to the joint agreement and then felt it incumbent to sell it to his controlling body.

There is some question as to whether or not this

---

[2] The General Motors bargaining relationship also takes place in a fish bowl. The country as a whole is the General Motors audience. At Studebaker the audience is only those directly affected by the relationship.

technique of bargaining as representatives is a clear index of where the real power of decision lies on each side. Thus, the two top officers of the company, the president and the chairman of the board, have been actually in a position to formulate and carry out labor policy in their direct dealing with the union within only a general framework provided by the board of directors. In the same way the union officials have not merely played a passive role in reflecting the wishes of the membership. They have also provided leadership in formulating demands and planning tactics.

The important thing has been that each side has always acted toward the other *as though* the ultimate source of power in decision-making was behind, rather than in the hands of, the negotiators.

A very interesting example of this point occurred when the vice-president in charge of production added an assistant to his staff whose primary responsibility was to take over some of the burden of industrial relations work centering in the vice-president's office. To the union officers this new man appeared to be different from what they had come to feel was a Studebaker management type. He seemed to be an unnecessary intermediary between union officers and the company vice-president. Moreover, he was a relative newcomer to the company, having less than ten years of service. Rather than make a personal attack on the new assistant the union took quite another course. Declared the union, he was there to report directly to the board of directors what the company and union were doing. How could he have ever come into the picture? According to the union officials the only power in the company capable of putting him in was the board. His very presence as a company representative with a philosophy that to the union represented a divergence from the expected standard was looked upon by the union as a threat to the collective bargaining relationship. Parenthetically, it should be added that the union officers told the new man, other company officials, and the authors about their suspicions. They made no secret of their displeasure with this alleged lack of confidence demonstrated by the board of directors in its bargaining representatives. Subsequently, the new company officer developed effective relations with the union officials after their initial distrust had been allayed.

Several consequences flow from this conception which management and union hold of their bargaining relationship. In the first place there has been a marked foreshortening of the bargaining chain. Too many bargaining representatives at too many levels of authority would play havoc with the system. Thus, it has been characteristic that although there were four levels in the grievance procedure, the top two were the only significant ones. These have been the levels respectively of the vice-president in charge of production and the top, i.e., the president and chairman of the board. Grievances appearing to be minor have sometimes been handled at these top levels. The industrial relations department of the company in fact has not had any centralized record of grievances until they have reached to the top two levels.

The short bargaining chain has meant that union-management relations have not been carried out by a group of officers on each side claiming to represent fully the company or union in all their personal actions. Yet this is precisely the practice in many companies where the foreman, the department head, the superintendent, etc., each constitute an inviolate link in the representation chain of management.

It has been recognized at Studebaker that too many steps in the chain of representation may be a block to immediate and decisive action on problems. For example, at the beginning of the reconversion period, in the normal confusion attendant upon such a major change in business operation, the top company officials were preoccupied with technical problems. Some confusion was inevitable in the handling of labor problems during a period when short-run uncertainty was widespread in the shop. A heavier than normal burden was placed on lower supervision to handle industrial relations problems directly. This is the comment of the union president at a bargaining meeting early in 1946:

> Everyone in this shop is just as suspicious as he can possibly get today, because no one will sit down and listen to them, and discuss their problems with them, and tell them whether they're wrong or whether they're right, and if they are right, take care of them.

Lower supervision could not handle these problems because it was too much of a change from past practice to be put in the role of making decisions always previously worked out at the top. Needless to add, the situation was temporary and the bargaining relationship was soon restored to its former condition.

A second consequence of this kind of bargaining of representatives has been the amount of time spent by top executives on industrial relations. This has already been implied above. The concentration of bargaining at the top levels of management has meant that small problems as well as large have been handled by the top people. This represents an interesting parallel to the centralization in the General Motors collective bargaining. It is evident, of course, that the reasons for the similar centralization are different in each case. The outstanding difference is that in General Motors centralization has represented a concentration in decision-making with a large measure of administration strung out in a long chain of the management hierarchy. In Studebaker decision-making and administration have both been concentrated at the top.

One of the logical consequences of this has been that the industrial relations department of the company has acted almost entirely in a staff capacity to the operating officials in dealings with the union.[3] It has been characteristic in the bargaining meeting to see the vice-president in charge of production, the general superintendent, departmental superintendents and the director of industrial relations on the company side of the table. The vice-president has made most of the company decisions after a lively participation by all members of the management group present. It was noted in examining the verbatim minutes of the bargaining meetings that the union bargainers have sometimes joined with the company officials in turning to the director of industrial relations for explanation of laws and their interpretation, as well as the entire maze of regulations and policy of all governmental agencies. In fact, one of the union officials pointed out that the industrial relations man was the "lawyer" in the bargaining relationship. This was not said in reference to a legalistic outlook on collective bargaining, but rather because he was the man who knew the most about such things.

FACTORS UNDERLYING SUCCESSFUL BARGAINING

A number of factors have contributed to the stability of the bargaining relationship at Studebaker. These can be summarized under three headings: mutual trust, sharing of information as the basis of decisions, and exclusion of outsiders from the bargaining relationship.

---

[3] All of the employment functions are under the supervision of the industrial relations director. These are "line" activities. We are emphasizing here only the fact that in labor relations the industrial relations director is a staff officer for the principal company executives.

Mutual Trust

Where individuals bargain with each other a minimum condition for their being able to agree is that a promise once made will be honored. There may exist suspicion of motives. But this point aside, agreement can still be reached if each party has a serious intent to abide by the agreement once made. There is considerable evidence that bargaining at Studebaker has met this test.

During the war, for example, a number of wage increases demanded by the union either were never processed to the War Labor Board because it was believed that they would be turned down, or they were sent to the Board and not allowed. With the end of the Board and the liberalization of the stabilization policy the union presented to the management a list of all such cases. "Here," said the union, "are the wage increases which you agreed should be made but couldn't because of the Board. Nothing stands in the way of adjusting these intra-plant inequities now." The implied promise of the company that it would adjust the wages when permitted by government policy was called. The wage increases were granted. A promise was fulfilled.

A second example of mutual trust has been the operation of the grievance procedure. Written grievances have not been required. The only formal record of the grievance discussion and decision has been the minutes of the bargaining meeting. But even this record may not contain the full discussion of the case leading to the decision. In many instances two members of the bargaining committee —one from each side—have met to settle the details of the case with only the results appearing in the record. Only when sufficient trust exists on each side can matters be handled in such an informal fashion.

A third example of this mutual respect has been the conscious effort of the company to work through rather than around the union officers. The company has not drawn a sharp distinction between "our employees" and "your union members." The two have been considered synonymous. For all practical purposes the company has always been willing to give support to a strong union organization by avoiding the consequences of this distinction.

Sharing Information

There has been a marked tendency for each side to use facts as the basis for argument. Thus the company officials have often given the broad picture to the union in the course of negotiations. For example, shortly after the war President Hoffman spent the greater part of several bargaining meetings giving the union the details of the company plans for the future. Particularly emphasized were the expansion plans of the company and the need for securing a stated portion of the total automobile sales in order that the company be secure.

Another example will make particularly clear this reliance on facts. The company raised the issue of production standards for crews loading autos into box cars. Production was low and the costs above prewar averages. A company official made detailed studies of the operation and then duplicated them at other companies having similar operations. At the bargaining meeting where the problem was discussed the company official meticulously laid out the facts as he had discovered them and drew the logical conclusions as to required production rates. Since the information gained at the other companies was confidential, the names of these companies were withheld from the union. This immediately brought down union suspicion on the entire factual basis of the company case. The union had asked for the company names in order to make an independent check of production at the other plants through their local unions. The withholding of this information ran counter to the union's expectation of freely exchanged facts. The net result of this particular bargaining session was to send the problem back for further study, even though the relevant facts were already known. Ultimately, after several more bargaining sessions, the production rate was established according to the company plan.

Still another example of information sharing occurred during the widespread suppliers' strikes of the immediate postwar period. It was common for the union officials to get in touch with the union officers in a struck supplier's plant and get facts on the strike and its probable duration. Furthermore, they often secured detailed information as to how soon deliveries could be made after work was resumed, etc. This information was passed on to the company to supplement what had been secured from the representatives of the supplier companies in order to provide a basis for predicting the effect of the strike on production at Studebaker.

One of the by-products of the emphasis on facts has been the requirement that all participants in this kind of collective bargaining be respected as technically competent. There has not been any place in this kind of relationship for the orator or the bluffer. You either knew what you were talking about or you shortly got to be a marked man. This has not meant, of course, that only a cold, dispassionate discussion has ensued every time management and union have gotten together. Each side has made use of warm words and emotionally charged phrases as the occasion has demanded.

On the management side, direct knowledge, rather than remote knowledge achieved through reports, has been one of the significant factors leading to an emphasis on a factual basis for collective bargaining. There has not been any remote control in the management. The chairman of the board, the president and all officials have been on the scene. They have participated directly in the collective bargaining. A decision can be reached in a matter of hours, not days or weeks. All the officials have known the plant in intimate detail, even down to minute individual operations. There has not been any need for reliance on long and detailed reports as a basis for decisions. Furthermore, and this is equally important, there has aways been extreme freedom of contact between union officials and all levels of management. As the union president stated: "I can pick up this phone right now and have an appointment to see Mr. Vance or Mr. Hoffman within the hour."

Sharing of information and using facts as a basis of bargaining has taken much of the emotional aspect out of the union-management relationship at Studebaker.

Exclusion of Outsiders

There has been a reliance by both union and management on their own ability to handle collective bargaining problems. Neither side has used the services of outside consultants in direct bargaining. For example, the union contract has not been signed by an international representative of the union as is customary in the UAW. In fact, with one exception, there has never been an international officer engaged in bargaining for Local 5.[4] Similarly, the company has never made use of consultants as bargainers with the union. The avoidance of outsiders is also evident in the fact that arbitration of unsettled differences has never been used. On several occasions offers to

---

[4] When the employment of returned veterans became a sizable problem, the national veterans' director of the union came into one bargaining meeting in order to explain what was being done at some plants. His role in the meeting was to provide information, not negotiate.

arbitrate have been made, but the solution of the difference through negotiation made it unnecessary actually to go to arbitration.

This allergy to outsiders participating as negotiators in the union-management relationship is not hard to understand. An outsider would take a tremendous amount of time finding out how things are done at Studebaker. By the time such a stranger learned the "Studebaker way" he would no longer be an outsider.

There has been a great reluctance on the part of both sides to wash any dirty linen in public. This is still further evidence of exclusion of the outside world. Management has never indulged in the luxury of giving a public spanking to the union. The union has never gone on public record with a condemnatory attack on management.

It should not be assumed, however, that this local has maintained only a nominal affiliation with the International. There have been frequent trips to Detroit for consultation with International officials. It is clear that these trips have been for business purposes and that the local officers derived considerable value from counsel received in Detroit. The significant thing is that they have not brought these advisors into the direct negotiations with the company.

THE PROBLEM APPROACH TO COLLECTIVE BARGAINING

The problem approach to collective bargaining can better be understood against the background of the initial relationship between the union and management. From 1933, when the Federal Local of the American Federation of Labor was organized, until 1937 when a contract was signed with Local 5, UAW-CIO, bargaining was carried out without a signed contract on the basis of a company statement of policy. The union was active almost exclusively as representative of individual workers on grievances. The company statement of policy remained relatively fixed and outside the reach of collective bargaining. Grievances were largely of a personal character and many of them represented the release of long pent-up resentments of individual workers against supervisors. The general superintendent characterized the situation in a bargaining meeting in 1945 when a grievance case struck him as similar to the kind that arose in the early period:

> .... what they're getting into there is what we had in here in '35 and '36—people who had a grievance of twelve years on back. Ninety per cent of the grievances we were going through for over a year were for people who had a grievance against a foreman who had been hopping them twelve years before. I sat in on those arguments and I know what I'm talking about.

The written contract shifted the emphasis away from the grievances of individuals to the consideration of group issues and problems affecting the entire work force. Thus, for example, in a study made of the grievance cases at Studebaker covering the period 1944–45 it was found that only 5.5 per cent of the cases involved individual's claims that they were receiving unfair treatment at the hands of their supervisors. In many companies in the mass production industries the proportion of cases of this kind is usually much higher, indicating that problems of individual dissatisfaction with the kind of supervision they receive are still very prevalent. For example, a parallel study made at one of the General Motors plants showed that 20 per cent of the grievances were based upon claims of supervisors' unfairness.

Just exactly how does this bargaining on problems work? Here is a typical example. During the war the army had inspectors and administrative officers stationed at the company to supervise the army contracts. This made everyone sensitive to possible criticisms which the army people might level at the way the company operated. A situation arose regarding early quitting by some employees. The vice-president in charge of production pointed to this problem at an early 1945 bargaining meeting in these words:

> We've tried to use every method to keep those people working up until a reasonable time of quitting, and every method that we've tried has been violently opposed. We even have conditions out there where these men will run their machines through the noon hour so that they can loaf in the evening, and we are going to be on the spot and it isn't going to be a nice investigation. I think we should do something to clean this thing up. I'm giving this to you [union] to give you some idea of what we are heading for, and I'd like to talk with you [union president] and whoever you want to bring with you the first thing in the morning over in the other plant and see if we can work out an idea to counteract this thing.

Remember he was talking about production workers on incentive rates. There was no long winded oratory about sabotaging the war effort. There was no "this is it, or else . . . ." attitude. Here was the problem, here was why they were concerned about it. Now, let's get together and wash the thing out once and for all. Even the fact that solutions had already been tried with no success did not bring forth a dissertation on management prerogatives in scheduling production and working time, and the like. The issue was ultimately resolved satisfactorily.

Detailed discussion of similar examples of collective bargaining follow but at this point we will summarize some of the characteristics of the "problem approach" so that these can be observed in the later illustrations.

Problem Solving vs. "Win the Case"

There has been no short-run "party line" displayed by either side around the bargaining table, designed to win now whatever the consequences. It was noted over and over again in the verbatim transcripts of the bargaining sessions that the management bargainers would look at the problem in hand from individual points of view. There was rarely any fundamental disagreement between the management men. At the same time there was no evidence that they had predetermined a line of approach to which they were all irrevocably committed. They all looked at the problem from the company side but they each brought to it some special knowledge or viewpoint. There was no evident embarrassment at the "thinking out loud" process before the union representatives.

The same sort of approach has been evident on the union side, though to a somewhat lesser extent. In most cases it has been the union which has pressed a demand, and hence had a prepared case for presentation. But very often the prepared line has been lost in the discussion and the union bargainers have resorted to the same thinking out loud as those on the company side of the table.

It would, of course, be quite the opposite if each side took a stand as a matter of principle on each issue. Then pat answers would be forthcoming in every situation.

Informality of Operations

The general purpose of the formal bargaining meetings held once a week has been to air the current problems. It has been a forum to get problems out into the open. The general basis of a solution may be worked out at these meetings, but more often the details have been established through conferences of smaller groups from each side. The union president and the vice-president and the divisional representative whose group is affected have joined with one or two of the management officials to work the problem out in detail.

This informality is an essential feature of problem bargaining. The purpose is to do the job expeditiously. A group as large as the combined bargaining committees totaling approximately twelve men is not flexible enough to get down to the minute details of cases. A few men working together can do this.

A further aspect of the informal approach has been the emphasis by both sides upon intent rather than legalistic interpretation of the union contract's written word.

When a major revision has been made in the contract, such as the publishing of a new edition with the latest changes, a joint conference has usually been held with the stewards and foremen to go over the document. The meetings threshed out the various interpretations of the contract clauses. In particular, the intent of any ambiguous phrases has been reviewed so that there would be general uniformity in understanding what was intended by the parties.

Observation has shown that there has been relatively little time spent in the bargaining meetings splitting hairs as to the meaning of words in contract clauses. In fact, remarkably little reference has ever been made to the contract. It seems to play a role somewhat like the Constitution of the United States. Everyone holds it as a sacred document, but few have more than a general idea of its specific contents. It was a rare instance where the union came in with a grievance charging specific violation of a contract clause. Part of this attitude has been built up in the postcontract conferences where the emphasis has been on general intent rather than specific wording.

Two Sides to a Bargain

The company has always recognized that it takes two to make a bargain. As a consequence it has often put the union on the spot to make positive proposals in settling a problem. Figuratively the management has said, "Well, what have you to offer in clearing up this thing?" This has often placed the union officials in the position of having to really dig for a positive solution.

Such management tactics look on the face of it like an open invitation for the union to assume management functions. Actually, the union officials have seldom accepted the invitation. This hesitancy has been based upon the knowledge that functioning as union officials is itself a full time job. As the union president stated:

> The company throws the ball to us a lot of times. We don't particularly like it. It's nice to feel that they think we're capable of carrying the ball. But we actually prefer to have them keep the initiative. It makes a lot more work for us if we get involved in much of this management business.

The union had one early experience in which it volunteered its services to management. In 1939, when the new low-priced car, the Champion, was introduced, the union went all out for its sale. Unbeknown to the company, a public relations man was hired and several advertisements were placed in the South Bend papers. Gist of the advertisements was that the good citizens of South Bend who worked at "Studebaker's" expected their fellow citizens to support a home town product. Merchants were suddenly made uncomfortably aware that their customers eyed their private cars with uncommon interest, especially if they weren't of a certain make.

The company didn't want its cars sold on this basis and succeeded in getting the union to bridle its enthusiasm for sales. With thanks for the effort, but an urgent insistence that sales should be left to the proper functionaries, the company won the union away from its direct action program. The cooperation was exemplary, but slightly misguided.

To Err Is Human

Neither union nor management has tried to take advantage of the other for one-sided errors. Such an attitude relates to the feelings of mutual trust which have existed in the relationship, and contrasts sharply with the prevailing practice in most collective bargaining situations where it is expected that each side will take full advantage of the other's errors.

For example, in examining three years of the bargaining record, only one case was found involving misclassification of a worker which resulted in back pay for the period of the incorrect job title. The union has seldom concerned itself with demanding the retroactive adjustment of an obvious slip or error, particularly if it has been convinced that the mistake was made with no ulterior motives.

The company has operated on the same basis. For example, when general plant inequities were being adjusted under the 1946 industry-wide eighteen and one-half cent wage increase, the union set forth the adjustments it wanted. Management took specific exception to a number of the requests pointing out that new inequities would be created. With painful clarity the company explained its position and accepted the union proposal with the written understanding that it was the last word on intraplant rate inequities. Precisely as the management had predicted, the union was back shortly with a new list of inequities for adjustment. In spite of the formal written agreement that the problem was closed (an exchange of letters had taken place) new adjustments were made from the unexpended balance of the inequity fund set aside out of the general wage adjustment.

It is almost as though the parties to this relationship, knowing the frailties of man, have realized that there should not be severe penalties for trying, if the intentions are honorable, but the efforts misguided.

Keep Bargaining Agreements Definite

The union has insisted that bargaining agreements be explicit and definite.

Two examples will make this point clear. It was agreed by the company and the union that certain of the shop clerks should be placed on salary and thus removed from the bargaining unit. After this agreement was in effect for some time, several of the shop clerks were still on the hourly roll, and hence still eligible for union membership. It was the union which came to the company and said, "Now look, let's get those guys on salary or we will be forced to sign them up in the union. We want to have everything clear cut in this shop, and those boys should have the same treatment as the ones now on salary." The company answer was a masterpiece of terseness: "They are on salary effective 8 A.M., this morning."

The second illustration concerns the actions of a personnel clerk. With reconversion, the foundry was put back into operation making engine blocks and other parts. Most of the former foundry workers had enough seniority to claim production or assembly jobs under the plant-wide seniority system. Few of them wanted to return to the foundry. An agreement was worked out whereby they went back to the foundry on a temporary basis to get things started and then later bumped into the department or job of their choice. For a period of about a week, a personnel clerk handling the assignment of these men failed to get their choice of a job recorded, and in some instances even failed to make it clear to the men that they could go back to the foundry on a temporary basis if they wanted to. By the second week his procedures were straightened out, after union protest. The union criticism centered on the fact that foundry men who were not given an opportunity to state a job preference on returning to work could take advantage of the situation. They had had time while working in the foundry to learn of the new jobs opening up and could thus ask to bump into the choice ones which might not have been their original selection. The possible jealousy between workers which arose under this situation was objected to by the union.[5] It was the failure of the company to have the proper procedure in operation when the foundry started up that gave rise to the difficulty.

The Problem Approach: Summary

These five aspects of the problem approach to collective bargaining serve as a guide in understanding this kind of union-management relationship. There has been no predetermined pat answer to a problem before it has been discussed jointly. The formal bargaining meetings have been used to air a problem with the details of its solution being left to informal joint working groups. Management has often put the union in the position of making positive and constructive suggestions in handling problems. A mistake honestly committed by either side has not forever plagued the offender as a constant reminder to play the cards closer to the chest. And finally, the union has wanted bargaining agreements definite and fixed, rather than indefinite and uncertain.

We have seen so far the relationship between management and union characterized as the "bargaining of representatives" in which mutual trust, sharing of information as the basis of decisions, exclusion of outsiders from the bargaining, and the concentration on problems, have been the principal ingredients. We have reason to believe that the favorable wage situation has been a necessary, but not a sufficient condition for the cooperative nature of the relationship. Let us now consider in some detail additional examples of bargaining at Studebaker.

---

[5] Under the plant-wide seniority it was mutually agreed during the war that a worker with seniority could not ask to bump more than once in six months unless he was laid off for lack of work. The agreement was designed to prevent constant movement of workers from one job to another.

HOW BARGAINING PROBLEMS HAVE BEEN SETTLED

The following case histories illustrate various aspects of the generalizations listed above. Each case centers around a particular set of problems and out of each can be drawn some of these generalizations.

"What'll It Take?"

During the reconversion period there was strong and open evidence that the Studebaker workers had a new slant on production speed and the amount of work which constituted a "fair day." The union officials made no bones about the situation. "The people out there in the plant are simply not going to work as hard again as they did in 1941. Neither you nor I nor anyone else is going to change their feelings about that." A number of times the substance of this thought was set forth by the union officers in the bargaining meetings. This approach was the rationale of union demands for individual wage increases or additional personnel on specific operations.

Three major incidents occurred in which the union made the flat assertion that times had changed and the workers were not going to work according to prewar standards. The foundry, the body shop and the motor lines were involved. The pattern of the union demands and the basis of settlement of the cases were essentially the same. We will consider here only the foundry case.

The initial manning of the foundry after V-J Day included former foundrymen whose seniority entitled them to more desirable jobs in the plant. Many of them wanted to get out of the foundry. The prewar production standards were re-established in the foundry since the production was almost identical. Numerous difficulties were encountered in getting production under way. When most of the technical problems were settled, it became obvious that the foundry was working below standard.

Dissatisfaction snowballed. The foundrymen began demanding a study of production rates, claiming the present ones were too high. The union officials supported these claims, seeking to demonstrate a basis for them in any bit of shop gossip purporting to show why work was more difficult or exacting than before.

The company's initial attack on the problem was to insist that no time studies would be made until a reasonable effort was put out by the men. Said the vice-president, "There is just no use talking about retiming those jobs until we are getting a reasonable effort from those men. We will not study the jobs until then." To buttress the argument on effort, the foundry foreman participated in the bargaining meetings, presenting comparative production figures, prewar and postwar, for identical items. Then the union took another tack and requested additional personnel in the foundry as well as several wage increases. Still nothing happened.

Meantime, production throughout the plant rose steadily to the point where the foundry became a bottleneck. The work effort was no better than before.

"What'll it take to get that shop operating?" This query by the vice-president started a chain of events which put the foundry back on its schedule. The union stewards held floor meetings with the foundrymen. The motor block lines were typical. Here the crews on each of two lines talked over the situation and agreed that so many blocks could be produced on each line. In addition, they demanded the adjustment of several wage inequities and several more people on the line, to be used particularly for relief. These proposals were taken back to the company.

Management agreed to a joint survey of the jobs and came up with answers that differed only slightly from the workers' production estimates, being a little higher on one line and lower on the other. Agreement was reached at the workers' production figures. After a few more days of operation trouble arose again. On the line where the workers' estimate ran higher than the survey, the men claimed that the survey convinced them that their estimate was too high. In further conferences it was agreed to lower the production standard slightly (about 3 per cent) on both lines to bring the high line down. The requested wage increases and additional personnel were also negotiated to a conclusion.

With these concessions the management took the flat position that the foundry situation was now settled. No more changes would be entertained since the whole situation had been thoroughly canvassed and all possible gripes had been considered and handled. Production reached a point satisfactory to the management.

However, increased casting requirements necessitated even more production from the foundry. The general superintendent was put in direct charge of this shop and told to get more production. After a check on the situation he reported that with certain changes in furnaces, capacity in excess of present demands was possible in the foundry.

This sequel is enlightening when viewed against the previous trouble over the workers' production effort. The easy course would have been to assume that even more effort would raise production. But an intelligent appraisal of the situation revealed that the remaining problem was a technical one.

This case is revealing as an illustration of the use of economic force by the union. There was open acknowledgement that a slowdown was in effect. The union was not going to order its members to stop the slowdown in the face of what it considered justifiable demands. The "what'll it take" attitude of the company finally broke the deadlock. From that point on it was a matter of the foundry workers, through their spokesmen, the union officers, coming to an agreement with the company on how to solve the production problem. It is characteristic of the "problem approach" that once agreement is reached to bargain that way, a settlement can be achieved. Note how close the workers' estimates of the daily production were to the estimates based on time studies. The difference between the two averaged less than 4 per cent. It is only when the atmosphere is cleared by agreeing to solve a problem that it becomes evident how small the differences between the company and union position can often be.

This case also illustrates how the company has operated the incentive plan. Management could have held to the adamant position that production items being identical with those of prewar days, the old production standards must stand. Actually, the company officials agreed to re-examine the production standards in the face of a situation in which the worker attitudes, the actual workers involved and some of the job conditions had changed. To this management there was nothing inherently sacred about time studies. In fact, the new studies in this case showed some downward revisions from the prewar standards to be necessary. And this management was willing to make the test in the interests of solving the larger problem of keeping production moving. Essentially the officials of this company have viewed time studies as a tool, and a necessary one, to an effective incentive system. They have not assumed that the incentive system exists for the benefit of time study techniques. In their view the incentive plan has as its basic purpose the stabilization of unit labor costs. Time study mechanics are for the purpose of helping to achieve this goal by providing certain objective measures as the basis for standards.

It is not our intention to leave the impression that the

corporation has been completely satisfied with the status of production in the plant. As a matter of fact, both union and management recognized in early 1947 that productivity was not satisfactory throughout the entire plant. In the case of the foundry, the motor line and the body line, certain initial postwar problems in re-establishing production were handled on a "what'll it take?" basis. This whole question of productivity will probably be the central point of future controversy between the company and the union when competition in the sale of vehicles becomes stiffer. In Chapter VII we suggest some of the ramifications of the problem of worker productivity.

The Iniquitous Inequity Adjustments

In preparation for the expected settlement of the 1945–46 General Motors strike and the establishment of the industry wage increase pattern, it was agreed in principle that one and one-half cents of the increase would be devoted to the adjustment of intraplant inequities. The question then became one of determining where the wage inequities existed in the shop.

The company put the issue squarely to the union, "You fellows give us a list of the rates that need adjustment and we will use that as the basis for discussion." The union held meetings of the membership, canvassed the stewards, and after some intensive work came up with a list of job classifications which should be adjusted, and the amount of the individual adjustments. A careful review by the management officials revealed two general objections. Some of the jobs were not entitled to a wage increase in view of the rates in force for other jobs in the same job families. Some of the proposed adjustments excluded groups of identical or similar operations which should be entitled to the same increase. In short, this set of adjustments created new inequities.

The entire situation was reviewed in careful detail with the union in a series of bargaining meetings. The union took an adamant stand that its list represented the desires of "the body" and therefore was mandatory on the union bargainers.

The industry wage pattern was finally established and the inequities came up for immediate handling. The company finally agreed with great reluctance to make the adjustment as requested by the union. Before the proposal was submitted to "the body" for final action, the management wrote a very detailed letter embodying its objections to some of the union proposals. Included in the letter was a job-by-job comparison of new inequities which would be created by raising only one of a pair of jobs. The company letter further stated that this adjustment would close the whole issue and no future request would be entertained by the company. It was agreed that the letter would be read to "the body" before a vote was taken on the issue.

"The body" voted to insist on the original union proposal. Then, several weeks later, in fulfillment of the management prediction, the union was back asking for new adjustments to straighten out some of the newly created inequities. The full one and one-half cent fund had not been exhausted in handling the first group of cases so that it was possible to make some of these further adjustments without additional cost to the company. The issue was finally resolved on this basis.

Throughout this series of negotiations the management consistently took the position that this one adjustment of the wage inequities arising out of the eighteen and one-half cent pattern was essentially a union problem. The full eighteen and one-half cents was due the employees, and if they saw fit to take a portion and use it to adjust individual rates, the company would go along.

Initially the company proposal was for an across the board increase for everyone. It would have been simpler that way. But the union insisted on its original proposals. There was grave danger that the plant wage structure would be further disturbed rather than stabilized by the union proposed adjustments. This was the point around which the company argument against the union demands centered.

In the end both sides got substantially what they wanted out of the solution to the problem. The union membership made its own decisions on how the money was divided. Not all union members benefited. But they all had the satisfaction of knowing it was their collective decision which determined the issue. For the company, letting "the body" decide on how to allocate the inequity fund did not cost any more money. All adjustments came out of the money originally set aside for this purpose. The benefits accruing to the company in terms of employee satisfaction cannot be measured in dollars and cents.

The Case of the Lost Shop Rules

Someone had thrown the book away and now the shop rules were lost! This was almost literally the situation towards the end of the war period. Somehow, in the course of developing the union-management relationship, a complete list of shop rules had become lost in the memory of management and union alike. With the wartime expansion of the work force and the hiring of many non-Studebaker workers, the problems of discipline became important again.

Particularly the question of gambling on company property was the subject of vigorous campaigns by a vigilant plant protection department. One amusing case arose in which the union seriously contended that several workers apprehended at gambling were unfairly caught. The plant protection man had violated all decency by spying on them from the roof of a building instead of manfully catching them from the ground. In addition, some of the foremen were resurrecting piecemeal an occasional rule they happened to remember as an *ad hoc* basis for disciplinary action. The union claimed this was unfair because the employees really did not know of the existence of the rule.

Both sides recognized that the solution would be to publish a new set of rules so that all employees would know what they could and couldn't do and the penalties for violation. In several of the bargaining meetings the union representatives needled the management men by stating, "We've been after you to get out a set of shop rules for several years. It's about time you did it now. We wouldn't be arguing about these cases if we had some rules which we all knew about."

So the management decided that a set of rules should be written up. The union president stated at one meeting, "O. K., you get something written up on that and we will submit it to the body for approval." There was no visible management protest at an invasion of a sacred prerogative. Actually the rules were never formally approved by the union membership. The shop rules, as finally published, were typical of any plant and would have met the approval of any management.

This case is typical of the union's insistence upon things being definite. As long as there were no standard rules to go by the union was forced to defend every discipline case on the ground of the culprit's ignorance of the "law." With the shop rules publicized the union could drop the obvious cases with no loss of membership loyalty. The violator simply had to take his just punishment.

The most interesting aspect of this case was not the way in which the problem was settled, although this in itself was typical, but the fact that the plant had operated for a relatively long period of time without a codified set of shop rules. The understanding of the Studebaker workers of right and wrong was sufficient to keep the shop operating with a minimum of infractions of common standards of decency. It was only the influx of many new workers that brought to a head the need for re-establishing more formal controls over employee's conduct.

The Bumping Bugaboo

The question of seniority and its relationship to production can be a most complex factor in operating a plant of 12,000 workers, like Studebaker. In handling this problem at Studebaker, many devices have been developed over a long period of time. Each one of these devices handled one administrative aspect of seniority. Yet not all were developed simultaneously. It is typical of the problem-solving method of collective bargaining that solutions grow and change with changes in a problem or some aspect of it. This case history illustrates that principle. At the same time this case is a good example of what might be called "union prerogatives" in the control of jobs.

It is not the purpose here to give the impression that the present development of the seniority problem at Studebaker has become the final answer for mass production industry. Some aspects of the bumping procedure in 1947 were still unsatisfactory to management. They were viewed as costly and unduly burdensome to smooth production by the top company officials. What is said here about the seniority situation at Studebaker reports only one stage in the solution of the general problem. It is significant, however, that the solution represents a compromise. There is reason to expect further compromises in the future. As a matter of fact, the tightening up on bumping procedures was one of the main issues in the 1947 contract negotiations. The union had already indicated a willingness to grant certain concessions in this connection to the company.

The union has always claimed that it has, without question, the best seniority clause in the automotive industry. Seniority is on a plant-wide basis with the exception of the engineering department, where the experimental work is done. The 1947 union president did not know why the company agreed to such a liberal seniority clause, but pointed out that it dated back to the earliest beginnings of the company-union relationship. A glance at the age and length of service statistics of the Studebaker workers, Tables 3 and 4 (see pages 121 and 122), gives part of the answer. The unusually high proportion of older workers with long service has made seniority a vital issue.

On the face of it, plant-wide seniority ought to be a major production problem in an industry characterized by regular seasonal fluctuations in employment. At Studebaker devices have been developed which have taken much of the burden of inefficiency out of the bumping problem.

How does the company view the seniority question? The words of a department superintendent in a bargaining meeting are revealing. "Seniority is your [union] problem. You can do with it what you want to. We're just looking for clarification on this, that's all." The statement was made with reference to the case of an employee who returned to the plant after having been loaned to another company under the war program of sharing skilled workers. This man wanted his full seniority restored. As a result of this and several other cases, the policy was established of having "the body" vote on each instance of claimed lost seniority before presenting the case to management. Seniority in this sense has been a property right of the union.

There are five adjuncts to the seniority system which have acted as checks and balances to control an unfettered plant-wide seniority scheme. Briefly these are: (1) cooperation between foreman and steward in policing worker's job qualifications when bumping rights were exercised; (2) a union imposed limitation on the frequency of bumping by individual workers; (3) a transfer pool through which information on all jobs has been coordinated; (4) the operation of the incentive system as a method of checking on worker proficiency; and (5) the short qualifying period for job proficiency which has imposed a requirement that individual workers qualify quickly or vacate the job.

There has been considerable cooperation between stewards and foremen in the handling of the bumping problem. In the first place, many of the older employees have been in a position to exercise bumping rights to "easy" jobs. This has been a regularized practice. The foremen and stewards have had understandings that such jobs were reserved for the older men. In the placement of workers they have acted accordingly. With respect to the question of skill the statement, in a bargaining meeting, by a steward is revealing:

> There's always been bumping out there—men would leave and we would get men in who weren't mechanics. They'd try to be but they'd take a crack at the job and we'd have to get together with the foreman and disqualify them. If a man couldn't handle the job we sent him out.

A man has had to be able to make out or else give up the job to another. Foremen and stewards apparently were able to agree on that.

Frequent bumping has not only been a burden on the company, but has made for uncertainty on the part of the work force. It was natural then for the union itself to raise the question of placing a limit on the number of times a seniority employee could exercise his bumping rights in a given period of time. Early in 1944 the union made a proposal that bumping rights should not be exercised more than once in six months, unless the move was made because of lay-off. The minutes of the bargaining meeting read: "[The union president] said that this question had come up at the union hall and the period of time mentioned at that time was six months." Although stemming from different motives, this union proposal was part of a solution to a company problem as well as a union one.

Another control device has been a transfer pool through which all job requisitions and applications for transfer pass. This clearing center has helped to coordinate the moves within the plant and has tended to reduce confusion.

The two basic control devices, however, have been the incentive system and the job rate progression formulae. The two are interrelated. On group piecework the new worker in the group has to be able to carry his share of the job or the entire group suffers. Pressure has been great to get the newcomer up to group production standards. On the individual piecework system, in a relatively short period of time the worker is expected to be earning above the classification rate. This has provided a quick check on his ability to make out on the job.

It is at this point that the job rate progression sequence becomes important. On group piecework, no employee, seniority or non-seniority, works more than two weeks until he starts participating in the group rate.[6] On individual piece rates the new worker gets the hiring rate or actual earnings (whichever is higher) for two weeks

---

[6] The union contract defines the first week as the week in which the job is started. It may therefore be less than a calendar week, if the employee starts on the job after Monday.

and then actual earnings; seniority workers get classification rate or actual earnings the first three weeks and then actual earnings.

It is evident that a worker must qualify on a job in a very short time. A group knows that the company puts just so much money into the work group to cover the classification rate of the members. Actual earnings above classification rate depend upon production in excess of the standard. The incentives get cut down if the group has to carry a worker beyond the qualifying period. The steward will soon know about such cases. The steward will, furthermore, be very much attuned to the skill requirements of the jobs in his jurisdiction and steer obviously unqualified workers away from skilled jobs in order not to incur the wrath of a dissatisfied group.

The plant-wide seniority has not worked perfectly. Particularly in a period such as the reconversion to peacetime production, when there were major changes in the production setup, a more than usual series of long bumping chains and consequent disruptions in the work force occurred. The result was company concern with the present seniority system. But with stabilization of production the situation settled, and the checks and balances listed above became operative again.

The control of seniority in the hands of the union has represented one of the vital areas in which the union has established a strong union prerogative. It exemplifies the kind of job control which the union has established in this and other areas.

The evidence indicates that the union has not abused its control over seniority by the arbitrary use of power. If anything, the evidence points to the conclusion that the union has made an intelligent effort to harmonize its objectives in the operation of the seniority system with those of management. Both sides have found the system a reasonably workable solution to a typical plant problem.

Another point should also be emphasized. It will be noted that there has been a functional relationship between the incentive system, the length of the qualifying period for a job, the cooperation of steward and foreman in policing worker's qualifications and in protecting "easy" jobs for older workers, the transfer pool, and the limitation on exercise of bumping rights. This relationship has made the seniority plan work. Any one of these features alone would not have been sufficient in itself. Other features which run at cross purposes to the plan might offer obstacles to its successful operation. One of the aspects of the problem approach is that eventually these functional entities get hammered out in the course of collective bargaining and they form little logical systems within the framework of the large union-management relationship.

In the 1947 contract negotiations the seniority question was a major issue. The union president indicated that several changes were conceded to the company to tighten up on "bumping." But the significant point he made was that the agreed-to restrictions on exercise of bumping rights were also beneficial to the union. He pointed out that the former system worked hardships upon those who were bumped and had created dissension in the union. This is an excellent example of how union and company to achieve different goals can come to close agreement on the means.

The Auto-less Auto Builders

Sometimes management is faced with the paradox of having to allocate limited product among an almost unlimited number of potential buyers. Such was the case when car production was resumed. One of Studebaker's most insistent group of buyers was its own employees.

Management's handling of this problem is an excellent illustration of securing a direct return for a concession to the union. The number of cars available for employee purchase was tied to the production rate and increased proportionally more rapidly than total production after the standard output was achieved. Thus, the distribution plan became a spur to production. At the same time, this case history reveals one kind of control which the union has established to protect the relative equality among its members and to minimize forces which might have tended to create divisions among the membership.

With reconversion, a short run of the 1946 models (modified 1942) was put through the plant in preparation for the big change to the 1947 line. Following the prewar practice employee purchases of cars on the '46 model were held to the peacetime average of 1 per cent of the production. Enthusiasm for the '47 models was high in the plant and everybody quickly discovered that the old jalopy was ready for the scrap heap. Morale in the plant suddenly hinged on the sales program to employees. The company argued with force, and President Hoffman finally got the union to agree to a run of cars for distribution to dealers as demonstrators. Then the question of employee purchases would be taken up.

On the day the agreed-upon number of cars for dealers rolled off the line Hoffman met with the union and wryly stated, "You can't accuse me of stalling on this issue." He proposed that the prewar 1 per cent figure for employee purchases be continued. "No," said the union, "we went along with you to get the dealers stocked but our people are now entitled to drive a decent car and we need a lot more than 1 per cent." The company raised its offer to 5 per cent with the union still balking. Then came the clincher. Five per cent would go to the employees plus one half of the excess over the normal hourly production rate. By this time several weeks had elapsed in the negotiations so the company agreed that the 5 per cent would be retroactive to the start of negotiations.

A priority system was established and the cars started to move to the workers. The priority committee was a joint union-management undertaking working with the industrial relations department in administering the program. By the last quarter of 1946 most of the back orders were filled and deliveries were being made shortly after receipt of an employee order.

Then a problem arose. It was agreed that no employee would sell his car for one year in order to prevent chiselers from getting a car to resell immediately for a profit. The union was particularly concerned about this because it didn't want any of the workers securing a high priority and then not using the car. The union insisted that a new committee be set up to pass on possible applications for sale prior to the end of a year. The company reluctantly agreed to the program realizing that there was nothing but moral force to keep someone from selling his new car if he wanted to. But to the union it was necessary to have this formal control in evidence, because without it the sense of justice of the workers might be outraged by the actions of a few chiselers.

Note the company's course of action. More cars to the workers, but only if it got more production. It worked during a period when production admittedly had not reached prewar levels. Note the union's concern for possible abuses of the priority system. It wanted and secured a formal mechanism of control in order to make certain that each union member had an equal break in the situation. This is another illustration of the kind of control by which the union has sought to maintain relative equity between union members.

STUDEBAKER AND LOCAL 5: SUMMARY

It should be evident that we are dealing here with a power relationship between a management and a union in which the use of economic force has been latent, but none the less real. The issues around which the power struggle centers have been quite different from those in the General Motors situation. At Studebaker the issues have been local to the plant. Studebaker, in spite of its size—12,000 workers in 1946—will not set a pattern for many other companies. It has been partially dependent upon the power centers of the country where the general collective bargaining atmosphere has usually been established.

The Studebaker relationship has been characterized by effective relations between union and company. This means that collective bargaining has been the "bargaining of representatives." Characteristically the bargaining relationship has been carried on in an atmosphere of mutual trust and with the sharing of information as the basis of decisions. Outsiders have been excluded from direct participation in the collective bargaining.

Problems have constituted the unit of action. The problem approach to collective bargaining at Studebaker has been characterized by the absence of a pat answer to a problem before it has been discussed jointly. The formal bargaining meetings have often been used to air a problem and to indicate the general outline of a solution, with the details left to smaller joint working groups. In this kind of relationship the union has been placed in a position of having to make positive and constructive contribution to the handling of problems, and not merely to play a negative, sniping role. Both sides have been willing to admit the possibility of honest mistakes and seldom have indulged in the luxury of riding the other for errors. Finally, the union has always wanted the relationship to give it a definite and certain solution to problems. In this it has been joined by the company.

What Does Each Side Get?

Does the way in which Studebaker and Local 5 work out their collective bargaining problems really satisfy the goals of each side? To be sure theirs has been a peaceful and stable relationship, but peace and stability in relations between union and management for its own sake is a rare luxury few can afford in our society.

The company officials feel that by and large they have secured something in return for concessions to the union. For example, one of the top officers stated:

> Between 1933 and 1939 our wage rates doubled in this plant. Yet our unit labor costs remained almost the same. The workers got most of the benefits of technological improvements.

Thus, the company during this period was able to increase wages without increasing its direct unit labor cost.

The evidence of the many cases cited points to a complete lack of management fear that the union has been out to "take over the management and run the plant." In fact, the union has objected to the company putting it in a position of having to "carry the ball" so often. The company has also secured something else out of this collaboration. There have been a lot more people concentrating on the solution of problems than only the specialists on the company staff.

Finally, and of importance, the company has had industrial peace. The no-strike record has been a valuable asset from the standpoint of operations and has played no small role in the public relations program of the corporation. The amount of time spent in collective bargaining by the top management officials may be viewed on the debit side of the ledger. But who can say with certainty that the vice-president in charge of production should have devoted his time exclusively to strict production problems? In this company, labor relations problems are production problems. At Studebaker the investment of the time of key officers in industrial relations has appeared to be, in reality, a very inexpensive allocation of resources.

On the other side of the bargaining table, union prerogatives have become a firmly ingrained part of the relationship with the company. There has developed a marked degree of union job control. There has been an air of strength and solidarity which has given weight to an opinion or course of action endorsed by "the body."

This kind of union-management relationship has not been without its problems. The very designation of it as "problem" collective bargaining highlights the fact that neither company nor union ever has secured continuous and complete satisfaction. Individual concessions or demands by either side can be a source of worry and concern and give rise to subsequent crises. The entire question of worker productivity is one such continuing concern. The relationship, therefore, has been dynamic in the sense that company and union constantly have faced new problems and solved them on an immediate practical basis, often recognizing that today's solution may lead to tomorrow's problems. The real stability in the relations between Studebaker and Local 5 has arisen from their joint determination to continue solving problems on a consultative basis rather than solving each issue through open industrial conflict.

Conclusions

PART FOUR

CHAPTER VI

The Significance of Bigness in Union-Management Relations

THE General Motors situation is an outstanding example of union-management relations in a "power center." We have used the term "power center" to describe situations wherein both the union and the company, by virtue of their size and strength, have a far-reaching influence on many other union-management relationships, if not on the economy as a whole. The use of the word "power" does not imply that either the management or the union has formal or legal authority to exert influence. However, the position of prestige, influence, and leadership of the parties is such that others tend to follow the precedents set or to adjust in some way to the decisions made at the power centers.

In the automotive industry, General Motors has been over the past ten years the most influential power center and consistent pattern-setter. Yet, Ford and Chrysler have on occasion also set broad patterns in their negotiations with the UAW. In automobiles, there are three labor-management power centers. In most cases two of the power centers—Ford and Chrysler—appear to have followed the basic pattern set by General Motors. But in some cases, precedents on individual issues such as wage settlements, union security and pension programs may be initiated at Ford or Chrysler. The industry as a whole, thus, tends to adjust to a complex of broad patterns set by the "Big Three," but the most significant patterns set by the "Big Three" have been usually, though not always, established by General Motors and the UAW.

LABOR-MANAGEMENT RELATIONS IN A POWER CENTER

General Motors has no formal authority to set prices or wage levels in the automotive industry. Since the corporation accounts for nearly half of the nation's production of automobiles, its pricing and wage policies inevitably influence the other automobile companies, particularly the smaller producers. General Motors, by virtue of its size and prestige is an economic leader in the automotive and related industries, just as United States Steel is an economic leader in the steel industry. Such corporations are powerful in the sense that their decisions greatly influence those made by others up and down the line throughout their industries and even other industries.

In its relationship with unions General Motors is powerful in still another sense. It has the financial resources, the economic strength, and the determination to offer stiff resistance to union demands. It is in a better position than the smaller companies to weather a strike. Up to now it has been a potent force in preventing the UAW from achieving some of its long-range goals. Thus, supplementing General Motors' influence as a recognized economic leader in industry is its influence resulting from its bargaining power on the labor front.

The over-all power of the UAW is dependent to a great extent on its strength in General Motors. It is difficult to get wage increases throughout the industry, for example, without getting General Motors to set the pace. The union's ability to wrest concessions from the smaller automobile and accessory producers depends upon its ability to take on the "big fellow." Once it gets the big fellow to go along, its bargaining power is increased.

Another aspect of the union's power is its ability to shut down a large corporation or even an entire industry. Since General Motors produces a large volume of parts for other automobile companies, a strike in General Motors could, if carried on long enough, cripple some of the other car manufacturers. Such a strike would bring a sizable segment of the nation's economy to a standstill. The ability of a large union to shut down an industrial nerve center is power of a high order.

The concentration of power in big corporations is an accepted characteristic of the American economic system. Parallel concentration of power on the labor side is now and probably will continue to be characteristic of the economy. The new labor-management power structures are apparently here to stay. Let us set forth briefly, then, some of the general observations concerning the characteristics of labor-management relations in a power center.

First, the very size and prestige of an organization like General Motors makes it a logical focal point for concentration of power on the union side. In the absence of formal industry-wide bargaining, General Motors has in practice determined patterns for wages, conditions of employment and other issues which are followed by a large segment of the industry.

United States Steel is an even better example of a corporation which is forced by circumstance to do a large measure of bargaining for an entire mass production industry. There are many other parallel cases of big companies playing the role of pattern-setter both in an industry or in a particular region, area or community. When a corporation is "out in front" in the collective bargaining arena, it necessarily assumes a responsibility which goes far beyond the confines of its particular plants. It is subject to pressures from many segments of the economy because of its pattern-setting role.

In this connection, it is important to remember that not too many years ago corporations in the mass production industries were the great open shop fortresses effectively preventing the unionization of workers. Today, they are the magnets for growing union organization; they are the real bastions of the strength and power of the CIO. In the mass production industries nearly all of the large corporations are now organized. The largest and most solidly organized and financed local unions, as well as a predominant portion of the voting strength in large internationals, are in these plants. Many small companies in the mass production industries, on the other hand, are not organized, although they usually match the wages and working conditions of the unionized corporations. In the future, as in the immediate past, the big corporations will continue to bear the brunt of union pressures. Bigness on the side of industry leads to bigness on the side of organized labor.[1]

A second observation is that bargaining between big unions and big corporations often leads to internal centralization of decision-making and policy determination on both sides. With General Motors, the UAW found that bargaining on a corporation-wide basis would best serve the union's interests. After the "Strategy Strike of 1939" and the NLRB elections of 1940 it developed a corporation-wide collective bargaining offensive. General Motors in turn was forced to develop a corporation-wide strategy of defense to protect itself against the "inchworm" tactics of the union. The master agreement made

---

[1] The reverse case is also true. In the coal industry, for example, region-wide and later nation-wide pressure by the United Mine Workers made a strong employers' organization necessary for purposes of collective bargaining. In any industry where the business units are small and they face as a group the unified power of a strong international union, bargaining on a multi-employer basis is often the only means of mutual protection.

after 1940, which has applied to all plants where UAW has had bargaining rights, has been negotiated by top executives of General Motors and top officials of the UAW. Thus, in General Motors, which has aimed to operate in accordance with the principle of managerial decentralization, labor relations have been a subject for common policy determination at the top. Likewise, in the UAW which has been noted for grass roots militancy and local union autonomy, centralized policy determination (exerted through the GM Department and the Reuther staff) has been developed to match the corporation's united front. A roughly parallel situation has existed in the case of United States Steel. From the outset the steelworkers' union developed a common policy at the top. The first agreement was made on a corporation-wide basis and the pattern has persisted.[2] In such situations, each side has been apparently impelled to centralize plans and strategy in order to provide a united front in its relationships with the other. Consequently, as relations between big corporations and big unions become more mature, it is logical to assume that the top level coordination of policy determination will be increased on both sides. This, of course, may make policy determination in big business more rigid and difficult; at the same time it is likely to accentuate the shift of vital decision-making responsibility in unions away from the rank and file into the hands of the top union officials. Relationships between big unions and big industrial empires tend to pyramid the influence of top officials in both.

A third observation is that the determination of policies in labor-management power centers is complicated.

---

[2] In practice, different agreements are in effect for the various United States Steel subsidiary companies, but their provisions on major issues are almost identical. The negotiation process, furthermore, is in reality on a corporation-wide basis.

On the union side, internal political rivalries between factional machines are likely to be intense because the stakes in the struggle over power are so large. On the employer side, decision-making may be complicated by committee systems, by differences of viewpoint between presidents of subsidiaries or managers of divisions, by confused staff-line relationships, and similar factors—all of which make decision-making a slow and unwieldy process. The individuals who sit around the bargaining table often are not free agents; they are, instead, focal points for reactions of all kinds from all quarters. The employer representatives must consider, for example, the effect of their decisions on the stockholders, the workers in their own plants, their competitors, and the general interest of the industry. The union representatives must consider, in addition to the interests of their own members, the effect upon the bargaining position of sister or rival unions. In negotiations, each side may be committed before the bargaining starts to programs which stem from protracted discussions and expedient compromises of conflicting viewpoints within its own group. There is usually an absence of flexibility, therefore, in the joint union-management decision-making process. This fact makes agreement much more difficult, but it is usually unavoidable in relationships of this kind.

A fourth observation is that the day-to-day administration of the contract must be fairly formal and legalistic if it is to be consistent. Procedures are necessary to both the company and the union. These procedures and precedents in the handling of grievance cases are important factors in the establishment of a "body of law" to govern the relationship between the parties. On both sides the lines of communication are long, involving many foremen and stewards. The distance between those who make decisions and those who carry them out is great not only in terms of geographical and physical location, but also in terms of status, experience, training, and outlook. As in large armies, communications both upward and downward must be systematized. As a result, human relations sometimes become "dehydrated." Respect for individual equities in some cases becomes subordinated to the observation of rules. Yet rigid procedures, rules, and clearly established lines of formal communication are necessary for any kind of orderly collective bargaining relationship between large corporations and the unions with which they bargain.

A fifth observation is that in labor-management power centers, the areas of conflict usually overshadow the areas of cooperation. The predominance of conflict stems in part from the concentrations of power on both sides and the consequent struggle for dominance and leadership. In 1945, for example, the UAW was banking its reputation and its bid for leadership in the national economy on a wage-price policy which it attempted to bargain out with General Motors. The corporation was fighting a battle to preserve its traditional managerial functions. It was constantly conscious of its leadership in American industry. It was, on this issue, fighting the frontline battle for principles in which the majority of businessmen believe. Similarly, in the steel negotiations of 1947 the United Steelworkers were carrying the banner for a great many workers in AFL as well as CIO unions. The smaller steel processing and fabricating companies throughout the land were nervously awaiting the decision of "big steel," which would, for practical purposes, determine their wage levels. In the power centers the issues are critical. The implications of the joint decisions are broad. Consequently, the pressures built up on each side are heavy.

The sixth observation is that the issues in labor-management relations between the "big fellows" usually have political overtones. In General Motors the management's knowledge of Reuther's plans for joint economic planning in the industry and broad social controls by government lies at the bottom of much of the opposition to the collective bargaining policies as well as the political programs of the union. Much of the union's antipathy to General Motors stems from the corporation's aggressive opposition to anything reminiscent of New Dealism plus its constant political pressure for restrictive labor legislation. Although political considerations in other power centers may not be so pronounced as in the case of General Motors, they usually play a vital part in nearly all collective bargaining relations between big businesses and big labor unions. In the steel and automobile negotiations of 1947, for example, the President attempted to persuade the big corporations to reduce prices so that large wage increases which might lead to more serious inflation could be avoided. At times the government has put similar pressures on unions to be moderate in pressing for wage increases. Since the outcome of negotiations between the corporations and the unions in the mass production industries inevitably has a profound influence on wage-price relationships throughout the entire economy, the government is likely to be involved in the negotiations.

The final observation is that so-called "free collective bargaining" over economic issues is usually impossible in labor-management power centers. Labor-management relations in power centers have ceased to be the private affairs of the unions and corporations involved. The emphasis placed by both General Motors and the UAW on "public relations" is a clear indication that both parties recognize that the community is vitally affected by their respective actions. The great "statistical offensives" which have been launched by labor and management in the past few years are designed as much, or perhaps more, to influence public opinion as to change confirmed beliefs of the parties engaged in collective bargaining.[3] In the labor-management power centers there is always pressure on the parties to take positions in negotiations which have strong public appeal. The public, as a result, is generally informed about these controversies, although it may be confused or misled by the barrage of propaganda aimed at it. Here again, "big league" labor-management relations show a significant departure from so-called "free collective bargaining." Inevitably, the public in one way or another has some influence at the bargaining table, if only in the capacity of an invisible onlooker whose confidence both sides want.

These six observations outline the characteristics of a "generating type" of labor-management relationship. Many of the same characteristics might apply to the case of United States Steel and possibly several other parallel cases in the mass production industries. It is obvious that labor-management relations in power centers of this kind must be sharply differentiated from collective bargaining in smaller units. In these so-called generating types the issues are broader and the stakes are higher. They are important nerve centers of the broad relations between management and organized labor. They really create much of the "industrial relations climate" of America.

SOME IMPLICATIONS OF BIGNESS IN LABOR-MANAGEMENT RELATIONS

The actual and possible impact of these new power structures on the American economy, as set forth below,

---

[3] In particular, reference is made to the "economic briefs" of the UAW and General Motors before and during the strike of 1945–46 which were widely publicized and expertly dramatized. Other examples are the "Nathan Report" of 1947 which was publicized by the CIO as a means of building up public support for wage increases, and the UAW report of 1947, *Wages, Prices, Profits: The Automobile Workers' Case for a 23½ Cent Wage Increase.*

is examined to establish guideposts for thoughtful deliberation and further analytical study.

One constructive feature of the growth of union power matching industrial power has been the constant pressure to improve and to protect the rights of individuals in industry. The establishment of the principle of collective bargaining and of formal grievance procedures is in itself a step forward in the area of worker rights.

The secondary effects of a strong union in a power center are equally beneficial. The improvements which have been made by big business in handling employee relations stem in no small measure from the threat of unionization and the fear of compromising managerial functions in union-management relationships. In large companies industrial relations are now a top management responsibility. Ten to fifteen years ago, a vice-president of industrial relations was a rare position in big business. By 1947 such positions were common throughout large enterprise. Few persons will deny that unionization is a potent management incentive for better employee relations. Within limits, therefore, the competition between unions and management for worker loyalty is a progressive and dynamic force in American industry.

Another positive implication is that opposing power concentrations in industrial nerve centers are probably preferable, from the standpoint of the public interest, to dominance by either corporations or unions. Although both General Motors and the UAW might have the economic power to restrict trade, limit production, or engage in other monopolistic practices, unrestrained use of this power by either party is likely to endanger its very survival. In both cases, the parties must weigh the use of economic power in the light of possible social and political repercussions. Large organizations, whether they be corporations or unions, are targets for political gunfire.

In the case of General Motors, the UAW has challenged the policies of the corporation. It has had an incentive to uncover and expose antipublic actions of the corporation. As a result, General Motors, constantly under fire from the union, has been faced with another limit on arbitrary use of economic power. The corporation, when charging that unions are "labor monopolies," has been throwing similar obstacles in the path of labor leaders who might use power in an arbitrary fashion. If there are opposing concentrations of both labor power and corporate power in a union-management relationship, each side is faced with justifying its actions and policies as being in harmony with our competitive economic system. Although these justifications may not determine actions completely, they indicate an increased sensitivity of the parties to pressures from each other.

When we examine the attitudes, beliefs, objectives and motivations of the officials of the UAW and General Motors it is obvious that there have been few reasons for the parties to create any sort of bilateral monopoly at the public's expense. There is little danger of collective bargaining degenerating into collective collusion against the public as long as each party is challenging the leadership and status of the other. No one would deny that General Motors and the UAW could exploit the public successfully if they ever decided that their mutual survival depended upon collective collusion. Anyone acquainted with the realities of this labor-management relationship over the past ten years, however, would be forced to admit that there is little probability of such a joint course of action.

On the other hand, the UAW, as we have seen, has advocated multiple-employer bargaining and joint economic planning in the automotive industry. If there were joint labor-management control over the production and pricing policies of the entire automotive industry, would there not be, in effect, an industrial cartel? Would not this be cooperative activity of a collusive nature? These questions are worthy of consideration.

If the UAW were able to induce the auto companies to establish a joint control board in the industry, the government in one way or another would probably be a party to the arrangement as the representative of the public. It would be virtually impossible for the government to stay out of anything so big and so influential as a production board in the automotive industry. Furthermore, the UAW, which has been the most active party in pressing for such an arrangement in the automotive industry, itself favors government participation in industrial planning. Thus, if the Reuther forces were to have their way, the end result probably would not be a private cartel but a publicly planned and socially controlled industry. To be sure this might lead to a basic change in the system of private enterprise; on the other hand, it would not be bilateral private monopoly.

In the opinion of the writers, however, there are few immediate prospects of even multiple-employer bargaining let alone joint economic planning in the automotive industry. The main reason is that General Motors has been unconditionally opposed to both and has demonstrated that it is powerful enough to checkmate moves made by the union in this direction. The other automobile companies have been of a similar mind. There would have to be a considerable change in economic conditions and in the balance of labor and management power in the industry before such far-reaching changes could take place.

The situation in the automobile, steel and other mass production industries is not similar to that, for example, in the clothing trades. In those industries, the concentration of union power has not met with concentration of corporate power on the employer side. There has been no General Motors or United States Steel capable of offering steady resistance to growing labor power. Consequently, the unions involved grew to be much more powerful than any individual employer with which they bargained. As a result, they have been a potent force in standardizing certain competitive practices on an industry-wide basis in these trades. Since these industries are not basic in the economy, however, the government has not had occasion to become a party in labor-management relations in this area.

A somewhat different situation has developed in coal. As in the case of the clothing trades, there has been no great power concentration on the industry side capable of matching individually the labor power wielded by John L. Lewis. During the thirties, the United Mine Workers became the dominant economic force in the industry. But because of the basic importance of coal in the economy, the federal government has been continually brought into its labor-management relations.

The situation in the mass production industries, however, has little in common with that in either the clothing trades or coal. In steel and automobiles, for example, joint labor-management planning of pricing and production policies in a power center would probably force the government to become a party to decision-making. If this were to occur in the power center, the immediate result might be industry-labor-government planning throughout the mass production industries. The large corporations have been aware of this possibility. Ultimately, of course, the government would probably soon emerge as the principal decision-making authority.

In situations like the General Motors case, nevertheless, there are dangers. First, any relationship which is so charged with suspicion, distrust and open hostility is almost certain to make both sides emphasize their points of difference rather than their mutual interests. This makes it more difficult to enlist the support of workers in maintaining or improving efficiency in the plants.[4] Nor can the adverse effect of work stoppages and prolonged strikes which may result from such a relationship be minimized. A power struggle between giants introduces elements of instability and uncertainty into industrial relations. The protection that the public might derive from the fact that the groups are competing with each other may be offset by the inefficiencies, frustrations and industrial warfare inherent in such a relationship.

Second, from the political standpoint, there are serious consequences in any kind of relationship which emphasizes class differences. In General Motors the political and economic cleavage between the managerial group and the worker group is strikingly apparent. This contrast, perhaps, has been more pronounced in the automotive industry than in the steel industry, for example, but it has been prevalent to some degree in most large corporations in the mass production industries. The effective unionization of the mass production industries has, for the first time, given a large section of American workers an organized set of class symbols. At the same time, this has tended to make more explicit the class thinking of management as a reaction to union demands and political activity. Explicit class symbols and attitudes have probably become more evident as a result of the open clashes between organized labor and organized management.

---

[4] In our study of General Motors, it was impossible to measure the extent to which efficiency was affected by labor relations. There were, of course, conflicting claims and charges by the corporation and the union. The great changes in production required by conversion to war production and reconversion, furthermore, introduced so many complicating factors that it was virtually impossible to get anything more than expressions of opinion on this subject.

The influence of power centers in the determination of wages and the setting of wage-price relationships has both positive and negative aspects. Wage determination is likely to be made in response to political as well as economic criteria. In periods of full employment and full production the pressure for wage increases in the power centers may contribute to inflation. In slack times the rigidity of the wage structure may prevent adjustments of wages to lower price levels. To the extent that general wage levels in a basic industry are increasingly determined by the outcome of bargaining in the power centers, the wage structure of the country is apt to become more rigid. Thus, to a large extent, wages are taken out of the area of competition even without formal industry-wide collective bargaining. The relative competitive position of plants or industries then becomes more dependent on managerial skill, technology, sales policies, and other factors.[5]

It is important to remember, however, that wages in such industries as automobiles and steel have been traditionally subject to conscious determination rather than automatic control. For practical purposes, United States Steel determined the wage movements in the steel industry long before the advent of the union. To a somewhat lesser extent, General Motors or Ford set the pace in the auto industry long before the appearance of the UAW and other unions. The principal difference today is that wages are determined by joint union-employer deliberation in the power centers rather than by unilateral managerial discretion. To some degree, furthermore, the

---

[5] The consequence of the impact of wage determination and pattern-setting in the power centers of basic industries is a very important and complex problem which has been given little thoughtful attention to date. The ramifications of this broad problem, however, are beyond the scope of the present study.

patterns set may be more rigidly followed throughout an industry as a result of the actions of the unions involved.

If we proceed on the assumption that big employers will be bargaining with big unions over economic issues, wage patterns will continue to be determined in large measure by the conscious deliberation of those who wield influence in these organizations. Unless the big corporations and unions are both broken up into little pieces, it is wishful thinking to talk about wages in the mass production industries being set exclusively or even primarily by the invisible forces of the market. In terms of the economic welfare of the nation the only possible solution to this economic issue (barring turning the clock back) is intelligent and responsible decision-making on the part of key leaders of industry and labor in the power centers of the mass production industries.

There are, fortunately, some indications that the leaders of big enterprise and big unions are conscious of the necessity for responsible exercise of their broad influence. For example, Alfred P. Sloan of General Motors has indicated that what the country needs is "a business policy that recognizes a responsibility far beyond that within itself . . . . one that accepts the fact that it is no longer sufficient to limit the horizon of the management of enterprise to the mere production of goods and services . . . . one that gives consideration in the policy phase of its operations to its relationships with the economy as a whole."[6] Walter Reuther of the UAW-CIO has repeatedly stated that a union must not seek to maximize the narrow pressure group interests of workers as producers at the expense of the community. A progressive union leader, in his view, is one whose responsibility extends to the community and the nation as a whole. Both seem to

---

[6] Alfred P. Sloan, Jr., *Importance of Jobs* (Detroit: General Motors Corporation, Nov. 15, 1944), 15 pp.

have recognized that labor-management relations are not merely the private affair of the parties involved.

Although few management or labor leaders today will disclaim this kind of broad responsibility, company and union spokesmen are prone to charge that one or the other is shirking such responsibility. In fact, at the bargaining table, in the press, over the radio, and before Congress management has been attempting to have labor convicted of irresponsibility and vice-versa. This is one of the reasons why the "labor problem" became the nation's most crucial domestic issue in 1947.

This issue is not merely a question of "why doesn't each side practice what it preaches." The trouble lies in the fact that corporations and unions have different standards for judging responsible action. Each side has a different concept of the ultimate goals of a free society.

Although both management and labor leaders are striving for a free society, their ideas of freedom are quite different. To management a free society is one which affords freedom for private enterprise, freedom from the shackles of government or union interference in making fundamental business decisions, and freedom of economic opportunity for those willing to undertake new ventures. This freedom, management asserts, makes it possible for private enterprise constantly to increase efficiency and productivity which is the keystone of economic progress. To union leaders and the majority of workmen, on the other hand, freedom is more commonly identified with security. To labor freedom means freedom from want, freedom from fear of loss of jobs, freedom from worry about injury, illness and old age, a guarantee of the right to employment at fair compensation, and a greater share of the proceeds of industry. Business wants an economy in which economic opportunity is safeguarded; labor wants an economy in which security is underwritten.

The most important function of collective negotiations between labor and management, therefore, is to achieve a satisfactory balance between the goals of economic security and economic progress. In the power centers of the mass production industries some positive steps have been taken in this direction during the past decade.

First of all, by 1947 there were indications that large corporations had accepted unions as permanent institutions in their plants. Although there was a desire to curb the power of labor and to restrict the area of collective bargaining, few large corporations were trying to smash unions. The great strikes in the mass production industries in 1946 were, with few exceptions, among the most peaceful in the nation's history. In our discussions with executives in the automotive and steel industries during 1946 and 1947 we encountered practically no one who felt that unions could be eliminated from their plants. Yet in 1947 the large corporations had the sympathy and support of Congress and a large segment of public opinion. They might have chosen to break up the unions in their plants. Instead, they agreed to wage increases and even, in most cases, to a continuation of the wartime union security provisions in new contracts. On the other hand, most of the union leaders in the mass production industries whom we interviewed did not share this view. They construed the effort of industry to curb union power and to restrict the area of collective bargaining as a more refined, yet none the less determined, method of union busting.

Our conclusion is that, although collective bargaining and unions have become permanently rooted in the mass production industries, the questions involving the status and power positions of the parties—in particular managerial functions, union security, and the scope of bargaining—were still the central issues in labor-management relations. The survival of unions was no longer a question; the main controversy centered on their power vis-à-vis corporations and the degree to which they could become partners of management.

In the case of General Motors the establishment and operation of the grievance machinery and umpire system represent a constructive contribution to joint solutions of problems throughout a complex and far-flung organization. The same observation would apply to other power centers such as United States Steel or General Electric. In the case of "big steel," moreover, there have been indications of much greater progress. In 1945 the United Steelworkers reached an agreement with the Carnegie-Illinois Steel Corporation (the largest U. S. Steel subsidiary) on the principles and procedures to be used in the determination and elimination of intraplant wage rate inequities and reductions in the number of job classifications. Although this action was taken pursuant to a War Labor Board directive in 1944, it nevertheless was a milestone in the collective bargaining history between the parties. Both sides have been, for the most part, pleased with the outcome. From the union's standpoint a more orderly and systematic rate structure adds to the workers' sense of certainty and security. From the company standpoint it makes for more efficient and productive operations. On both sides there has been a feeling of accomplishment in making some progress toward working out one of the thorniest problems in the industry. In their 1947 United States Steel contract, furthermore, the parties reached agreement in principle on severance pay in event of lay-offs due to permanent closing of a plant or department. They also agreed to set up joint safety committees in each plant to advise with plant management concerning safety and health matters. They agreed to establish a joint committee to study seniority practices in effect throughout the plants and to recommend improvements in job administration consistent with the objectives of the parties which were set forth as "efficient operations, protection of the employees and cooperative employer-employee relationships." They further agreed to work out jointly details of an employee social security program. Finally, provision was made for a joint appraisal every three months of problems which might arise in the application, administration and interpretation of the contract.

Although the provisions set forth above relating to the United States Steel contract do not greatly expand the scope of labor-management relations, they nevertheless indicate a desire on the part of both the union and the corporation to make collective bargaining work. They constitute steps in the direction of harmonizing the goals of economic security and economic progress. In this connection a statement summarizing the purpose and intent of the 1947 United States Steel agreement may be significant: "By such arrangement the parties believe that they, as men of good will with sound purpose, may best protect private enterprise and its efficiency in the interests of all, as well as the legitimate interest of their respective organizations within the framework of a democratic society in which regard for fact and fairness is essential."

In 1947, however, the really fundamental problems of balancing the quest for security and the need for progress still faced labor, management, and the nation. There was the problem of building up a much more adequate and comprehensive system of social security. There was the problem of developing within unions and management alike a more complete recognition that a higher standard of living for workers is dependent upon increasing the efficiency and productivity of industry. There was the problem of finding ways and means of providing steadier employment and assuring workers of an adequate yearly income—a problem to which big corporations and big unions were really giving intensive study in 1947. Some progress was being made toward these objectives, but the power struggles between large corporations and large unions tended to make a factual approach in collective negotiations difficult and complicated.

CHAPTER VII

The Nature and Scope of Constructive Union-Management Relations

THE Studebaker case represents a practical working model of what we term "constructive union-management relations." Such relations are achieved when a union and a company harmonize divergent goals into an effective working agreement. Constructive relations do not mean the absence of actual or potential conflict; they do not imply that labor and management have common goals. With constructive union-management relations both parties find in collective bargaining a means of at least partial achievement of their respective goals. Agreements arrived at in this kind of union-management relationship are generally consistent with the broad interests of the community and the nation.[1]

A significant aspect of constructive union-management relations is the ability to harmonize divergent goals and achieve an effective basis for working agreements. Employees as a group are not immediately interested in company profits as such. Business management is not primarily interested in the security of its workers as such. Each group looks at a business enterprise in terms of what

---

[1] It is important to point out that collaboration between companies and unions has resulted in some cases in collusive agreements made at the public's expense. There has sometimes been a harmonizing of divergent goals in some union-management relations which have bordered on racketeering. Naturally, such relationships could not be called "constructive" as we have used the term here.

it gets out of it. If unions and management accept the continued existence of our present enterprise system as the framework within which they must deal with each other, then at some point the quests for worker security and the economic progress of the business become closely related. At some stage unions become concerned with profits or losses because of the bearing they may have on employee security. Similarly, employee security in so far as it leads to higher morale and greater productivity may become an important consideration to a management conducting a profitable business.

The achievement by both union and management of some of their respective goals is important to the development of a constructive relationship. (The company expects solvency and at least reasonable profits in the long run. The union expects some economic gains and the maintenance of its independence from management as an organization. It would be rather meaningless for union leaders to talk about compromises with management if they start with nothing tangible in their own hands. Compromise under such circumstances would be tantamount to capitulation.

It is important to note that "constructive union-management relations" are something quite different from "union-management cooperation." Union-management cooperation is generally defined as a conscious joint effort to increase efficiency and productivity. To management officials this means that the union is cost conscious and efficiency minded. To union officers and members it means that management is willing to take union leaders into limited partnership in making key decisions affecting the production in the plant. These are broad expectations each side has of the other and require a fundamental change of policies and goals by both labor and management. Union-management cooperation on production is an ideal. Being an ideal, it is never fully achieved. Instances of such cooperation, however, are usually acclaimed as an advancement towards industrial peace and general economic well-being. But immediately questions arise in the minds of many union and company officials as to whether such cooperation is really a forward step. Some persons in trade union ranks hold that a union "sells out" through cooperation with management. Others from the ranks of management view joint control of the work force in a business enterprise as a dangerous step in the direction of eventual union or social management of industry. In defense, business leaders rally around the battle flags of "management prerogatives."

The relationship between the Studebaker Corporation and Local 5 of the UAW has not resulted in joint efforts to increase efficiency. It is not, therefore, an example of union-management cooperation. For this reason the relationship at Studebaker has not been in any sense spectacular. There have been no sensational "conversions" of company or union officials. At Studebaker the parties have simply hammered out over a period of years a practical, realistic and stable method of getting along with each other in which both sides have confidence and from which each has secured reasonable satisfaction.

ELEMENTS OF CONSTRUCTIVE UNION-MANAGEMENT RELATIONS

To provide an indication of some important phases of constructive relations between union and company, it is desirable to consider briefly eight observations stemming from the Studebaker relationship. These observations are a summary of the distinguishing features of union-management relations at Studebaker. It is necessary to point out, however, that the Studebaker case is not an example of ideal constructive union-management relations. No one case ever is. However, the Studebaker history is significant because it shows how constructive relations can develop between a fairly large company and a local of a strong and militant mass production union.

The first observation is that labor relations at Studebaker have been greatly influenced by the comparatively tenuous competitive position of the company. Union organization started when the company was in receivership. Management's need to keep the plant operating, while strengthening its competitive position, was an important initial consideration in its selection of the policy of working with rather than fighting the union. Once having accepted the union, the management found that it could be an asset in running the business on a sound basis.

To members of Local 5, UAW, the ability of the company to maintain and enhance its competitive position has been a matter of crucial concern. Studebaker is the principal employer in South Bend, and the majority of the jobs in the community are thus dependent upon the company's prosperity. There are no alternative places of employment in the area capable of absorbing an unemployed Studebaker work force. At the same time the workers are rooted to the community by ties of home ownership and long-time family and group associations. The union, the employees and the community, consequently, have been vitally interested in the economic health of the Studebaker Corporation.

The second observation is that Studebaker has operated generally within the economic environment created by the large automotive companies such as General Motors. The price and wage patterns set by the large Detroit corporations have been the yardsticks for collective bargaining at South Bend. Each side has recognized that it must operate within economic limits set by bargaining between the large corporations and the international union.

Therefore, there has been a narrowing of the range of possible differences between union demands and company offers. The issues to be resolved have been mostly local plant or community problems. The relationship has not been complicated by power struggles and differences of opinion over national economic policies.

The third observation which stands out with great sharpness is the stability and security of the union. Local 5 has not been forced to compete with the Studebaker management for the allegiance of employees. Management has never fought the union. The company apparently has preferred to communicate with its employees through a strong and ably led labor organization. It has taken pains to build up the union in the eyes of the workers. Nevertheless, though loyal to the union the workers still look upon the company as "the most desirable employer in the community."

The union's secure status, however, has been built upon more than employer acceptance. Local 5 has acquired considerable control over jobs. The employees have been quite aware of the influence and power of the union leadership in dealing with the management on matters of this kind.

At the same time, the union has been secure in the community. Local 5 has been generally regarded as a progressive and stable social and economic institution in South Bend. The organization has been accepted as a permanent part of community life. This community recognition has been linked in part with the active participation by the union and its representatives in the civic bodies, social agencies and welfare activities of the community.

The union has also been secure because of the stability of its internal organization. There have been no really bitter factional quarrels within the union. A greater than usual percentage of the membership has participated directly in union activities, and the membership has played a relatively active role in determining union policies.

At every point where the union's status has been involved—in relation to management, the community, or its membership—this status has been high.

The fourth observation is that the management structure is simple and relatively informal. Studebaker is a fairly large company. Yet the rigid lines of communication and levels of authority which are usually characteristic of large organizations have never been developed at this company. The formality of organization necessary for administrative efficiency in a big company has largely been avoided. This factor has important repercussions in labor relations. It has promoted direct participation by top executives in collective bargaining. In particular it has sensitized top officials to the practical shop aspects of labor relations issues.

The fifth observation is the prevalence on both sides of the bargaining table of a "problem solving" approach to labor relations. As a result, collective bargaining issues have seldom been solved by reference to rigid policies. Major emphasis has been placed on the substance of the problems in hand, and relatively little consideration has been given to application of fixed principles.

Attention to these substantive aspects of collective bargaining is of great importance in developing constructive union-management relations. In much of the literature on industrial relations there is constant reiteration of the need for putting collective bargaining on a factual basis. The Studebaker case indicates that factual collective bargaining is promoted when both sides are willing to bargain on a problem solving basis. When company and union admit that neither has ready-made solutions to all problems, the process of negotiation can be carried out in a constructive manner.

A sixth observation is the importance of attitudes and techniques which are a part of this kind of relationship. The following attitudes appear to stand out clearly:[2] First, collective bargaining has been looked upon as a process of solving problems rather than winning cases. Second, both sides have recognized that it takes two to make a bargain—that a problem is not fully examined until all proposals and counter-proposals have been given consideration. Third, both parties have realized that perfection is an impossible goal and that union and management must both be flexible enough to accept the possibility of errors in judgment or action committed by either party without ulterior motives. In this connection, the test of sincerity most often applied by both sides has been to observe the willingness with which an error is admitted and corrected.

Coupled with these three important underlying attitudes are two significant techniques. First, collective bargaining business has been transacted in an informal manner. At the same time both union officers and company executives have been convinced that bargaining agreements must be kept definite and explicit to insure that an agreement has actually been reached and to simplify administration of a point settled through bargaining.

The seventh observation about the Studebaker case is that formal procedural devices, as distinct from attitudes and techniques of interaction between union and management, are relatively unimportant. Little time has been wasted on such problems as what kind of committees shall be set up, who shall serve on these committees, what is the scope of such joint activities, etc. The Stude-

---

[2] These points can only be listed here. They are discussed fully in Chapter V, pp. 146–59.

baker case presents convincing evidence that procedural devices are much less important than the over-all character of the union-management relationship in determining the kind of collective bargaining which will prevail.

The final observation is that the relationship between Studebaker Corporation and Local 5 represents a fairly even balance of power rather than a "sweetheart agreement." In spite of the record of industrial peace, the union has been ready to use militant tactics if necessary. The management, furthermore, has apparently recognized that a showdown might become necessary some day. The possibility of strikes, slowdowns and lockouts has always had an important influence on the decisions made by both sides. Each side has had respect for and considerable fear of the power of the other. Although there has never been a real test of power, each side has been governed in its actions toward the other by a feeling that there has been an approximate balance of power between them. During the years of their bargaining history, however, both sides have chosen acceptable compromises to the risks inherent in industrial warfare. Issues involving the status of the parties, which have led to continuous conflict in General Motors, have been resolved to the apparent satisfaction of the Studebaker management and the officials of Local 5.

These observations set forth the distinguishing characteristics of the type of constructive union-management relations developed at Studebaker over the years.

IMPLICATIONS OF CONSTRUCTIVE UNION-MANAGEMENT RELATIONS

At the present time we have no way of knowing how widespread constructive union-management relations are throughout industry. The cases involving extreme conflict or spectacular cooperation are usually the most extensively publicized. Yet there are probably thousands of instances where unions and companies are making collective bargaining work in a satisfactory manner.

It is unrealistic to expect labor and management to have the same goals. At the same time, it is necessary to lay the ghost of the commonly held belief that company and union can live peacefully with each other only when they are striving towards common goals. It was pointed out in Chapter VI, for example, that one of the basic labor relations dilemmas is the conflict between the worker's goal of individual security and the management's goals of efficiency and freedom in directing an enterprise. Professor Bakke has pointed to the general conflict of goals as follows:

> I could not avoid a major conclusion . . . . both management and union leaders were expecting the other to behave in a way which each believed was impossible if they were to survive. Each was expecting peace on terms consistent with his own sovereignty. Management anticipated peace when the unions became the kind of organizations which fitted in with management's conception of the principles of workable industrial relations. Union leaders expected peace when management accepted and bargained in good faith with unions as they were. . . . . The plain fact is that management's convictions about sound management and the union leader's convictions about effective unionism don't fit together at important points.[3]

Under what circumstances can one-sided approaches in labor-management relations be modified? In what type of situations is there most likely to develop a willingness on the part of each side to accept the status of limited sovereignty—the limits being imposed by the interaction of union and management with each other?

Our studies lead us to believe that constructive union-

---

[3] E. Wight Bakke, *Mutual Survival: The Goals of Unions and Management* (New Haven: Labor and Management Center, Yale University, 1946), p. 2.

company relations are most likely to develop outside the labor-management power centers. Outside the power centers company and union bargain with each other within the limits of economic patterns already established and over which the local union and management have no direct control. Both sides become accustomed to looking outside the scope of their negotiations for important guideposts in contract negotiations. Both sides clearly recognize that their respective sovereignty to make collective bargaining and business decisions has already been limited in important respects by virtue of dependence on leadership in policy formation and action at the "generating centers" of the economy. For this reason constructive union-management relations are likely to be found in small or medium sized companies.

The fact that a constructive relationship between company and union is most likely to develop in medium size and small companies may have important economic implications. In the case of marginal concerns a stable collective bargaining situation may be a crucial factor in continuation of the business. This may become particularly true if collective bargaining reaches the "problem approach" stage and company and union can bargain with each other in the light of the reality of the company's financial and competitive position. But the advantage is not limited solely to marginal concerns. A small, prosperous firm may further enhance its strength by minimizing the costs of labor strife and worker dissatisfaction through constructive relations with its union. In both kinds of situations the small or medium size firm may be in a position to develop and turn a constructive relationship with its union into an important competitive asset. Such a course of action is much more difficult, in cases such as General Motors, where the conflict between union and management power is usually predominant.

Constructive Relations: Advantages and Problems

When we consider the implications of constructive union-management relations in the actual plant situation there are some obvious advantages as well as several problems involved in establishing such a relationship. A realistic appraisal of the advantages as well as obstacles is important.

The Studebaker situation clearly indicates that there are advantages in a work force which has a feeling of security. In this case the fear of oppressive supervision and arbitrary action by management has been effectively minimized. The favorable employee attitude toward the company has not resulted from "morale building programs" or formal company action to "sell" management to the workers. Confidence in the company has been an outgrowth of day-to-day application of good personnel management through relations with the union. It is, of course, difficult to measure employee good will in dollars and cents, but the general interest of management in favorable worker attitudes indicates the high valuation placed by business executives on this factor.

Under constructive union-management relations the potentially unstable position of foremen and lower supervisors may be exposed. There exists a potential threat to the authority of the supervisor which may develop if the union officers short-circuit supervision in favor of dealing directly with top management. Executives may also wittingly or unwittingly place the foremen "in the middle" by dealing directly with the union at the top levels. Foremen are likely to construe this by-passing as an attack upon their status and develop hostility towards the union and suspicion of management.

Truly constructive relations require a willingness of persons throughout the entire management structure to join with members of equal rank in the union in working out mutual problems together. It is necessary for each foreman to establish close working relations with his steward, and so on right up to the top officials on each side. Underlying this willingness to work with union officials must be the conviction that such a relationship is desirable and actively backed by top management. Furthermore, each supervisor has to be reassured that the inclusion of union officers in decision making, formerly left pretty much in the supervisor's own hands, does not undermine the responsibilities inherent in his job. Unless such understanding on the part of lower supervision is achieved, constructive union-management relations are likely to be found in skeleton form only at the top levels of management and union, with decisions reached by top company and union officials being carried out by foremen and stewards as a matter of directive from above. Thus, in one case in the steel industry, the operating head of the company called in all his supervisors and made it clear to them that they were subject to dismissal unless they actively supported a newly inaugurated program of working with the union. Normally, however, the confidence of supervision in such a program is better developed by a less authoritarian approach.

There is a positive side to the supervisor's problem of living with the union in a constructive manner. A camaraderie of foreman and steward may very well serve to relieve some of the tension the foreman feels from being "in the middle." The foreman and the steward with whom he deals are both of the same relative rank in their respective organizations. There is likely to be an approximate equality of general status of foreman and steward which can lead to a sympathetic appreciation of each other's position. This situation can result in freer communication between the two.

Under a regime of truly constructive relations between company and union all channels of communication within both the company and union organizations are utilized to the fullest extent. It is necessary to emphasize that such communication requires more than the written word or the formal spoken command. Much of the vital activity in a plant is based on informal exchange of ideas among those immediately involved in a particular operation or plan of action. When the affected group has been broadened out to include workers and union officials as well as management personnel, a greater range of ideas and interests can be brought to bear on a problem. In its positive aspect the freedom with which suggestions and advice are offered by workers and union officers and accepted by management can constitute a marked advance over the more traditional and formal type of company suggestion system. In the Studebaker situation the informality of the bargaining procedures and the greater than normal participation of the members in the affairs of the union constitute evidence that channels of communication have been quite effectively utilized.

Constructive Relations and Union-Management Cooperation

Constructive union-management relations may lead under certain conditions to active collaboration in increasing plant efficiency—in other words to union-management cooperation. However, union-management cooperation, though spectacular, is usually short lived. Most of the experiments in union-management cooperation have had their origin in a crisis of some kind. In a few cases cooperation has resulted from a desire on the part of a company and union to achieve some specific immediate objective without the stimulus of forces threatening either side.

In the Naumkeag Steam Cotton case, for example,

the union and management cooperated to increase worker productivity in order to avert company bankruptcy.[4] The famous case of cooperation in the Baltimore and Ohio Railroad shops likewise started with the threat of loss of jobs by the employees involved. The same kind of crisis cooperation was fairly common in some small steel companies in the late thirties. Such cooperation may become more common again in the future if small companies in the mass production industries find themselves hard-pressed in meeting the pay scales negotiated by big unions and big employers in the power centers.

The reasons for the crisis character of cooperation on production problems are fairly evident. Normally, management assumes full responsibility for maintaining the technology of production. Only when a bottleneck develops which company technicians are unable to solve will there usually be any inclination to turn to the workers or union for assistance.[5] During the war, for example, labor and management actively cooperated to improve the technology of war production. On the other hand, management is always interested in increasing the work effort and productivity of employees. But on that point, there may be strong worker and union opposition to an alleged "speed-up." Again, success in increasing worker effort usually involves a crisis situation in which the workers and union feel threatened with loss of jobs or earnings, and are willing to engage in active cooperation with management.

There is a very excellent illustration in the recent literature of wartime cooperation on production which

---

[4] R. C. Nyman and E. D. Smith, *Union-Management Cooperation in the "Stretch-Out"* (New Haven: Yale University Press, 1934).

[5] Golden and Ruttenberg have given numerous illustrations of cooperation on technological aspects of production problems in *The Dynamics of Industrial Democracy* (New York: Harper & Bros., 1942).

was initiated in an unusual manner. We refer to the bargaining relationship at the Lever Brothers plant at Toronto, Canada, involving Local 32 of the International Chemical Workers Union (AFL).[6] In this case the union pressed for a wage raise in return for its promise of increased operating efficiency to the point where the total wage bill per unit of output would be the same as before the increase was granted. The company was extremely skeptical of the possibility of such an offsetting increase in productivity. Lever Brothers agreed to start paying the higher wages only after a joint union-management production committee had been able to install its efficiency recommendations, and output had actually risen by the required amount. (It was also necessary that the Canadian War Labor Board approve the wage raise—which it did only after considerable delay.) The union gambled that production could be increased. Its membership worked under improved conditions of output for six to nine months before the wage raise was granted. The gamble was won, but the victory for permanent joint consultation was not. As the investigator, Dymond, candidly pointed out, the joint production committee stopped functioning and the union's request for joint study of certain issues like sickness and accident pay has been politely turned aside by the management. Furthermore, the company has been unwilling to establish a definite plan for sharing the savings of any future technological advances made in the plant. There apparently has been no incentive for the company to consider continuing joint activities with the union as a permanent feature of managerial functions.

We cite this case because it illustrates the temporary

---

[6] W. R. Dymond, "Union-Management Cooperation at the Toronto Factory of Lever Brothers Limited," *Canadian Journal of Economics and Political Science* XIII, No. 1 (Feb., 1947), 1–42.

basis of some union-management cooperation schemes. However, the end result may be a more permanent and lasting constructive union-management relationship as appears to have happened at the Lever Brothers plant.

This kind of crisis cooperation may in some instances end in failure. In the Naumkeag case an elaborate co-operation scheme was discontinued and resulted in the downfall of the union leaders who collaborated in instituting the "stretch-out." In a great many of such instances, however, active collaboration seems to die out after the crisis has past, although the company and union may continue to get along well together in a less spectacular way. In short, union-management cooperation on production problems which is a relatively temporary condition is likely to evolve from, or to revert to, what we have described as constructive union-management relations.

Why is it that union-management cooperation to increase worker effort and productivity is likely to be of temporary duration? We have in the Lever Brothers and Naumkeag Steam Cotton cases a very clear-cut description of what occurs. Work loads may be increased, number of workers may be reduced, wage rates may be cut, and downgrading of present employees may occur. Employees are likely to oppose such moves because they feel there is a "speed-up" or "stretch-out." Worker resentment to necessary changes is likely to be directed at the union officers who collaborate with management. The position of the union leader, who must take joint responsibility with management for the changes being made, may become very tenuous. Thus, an element of instability is created in the relationship of union leaders to their membership.

When union leaders agree to cooperate on production problems, there has to be a pretty clear understanding on everyone's part of just exactly what the union secures out of such action. It may be the very preservation of jobs in the face of possible closing of a plant or department. It may be a wage raise based on increased output, as in the Lever Brothers case. It may be the protection of existing wage rate levels in the face of widespread wage cuts. Whatever the issue, there has to be some immediate positive value to the union and its membership in the sacrifice (from their viewpoint) which is often involved in increasing productivity.

Equally thorny problems are faced by management in working jointly with the union to solve problems of worker productivity. The question is never as simple as a mere plea by management that more effort must be applied by the workers to increase production. Generally some kind of consultation between union and company takes place during which concrete action is agreed upon. The management decisions affecting the joint plan of action are usually influenced by the following considerations. There is first of all the question of speed in decision making. Some production decisions have to be made rapidly and may lose their effect if an unusual amount of time has to be spent on discussion and negotiation. Second is the matter of managerial know-how. There are technical decisions to be made, often requiring engineering or scientific knowledge, which must be handled by management's trained specialists. The problem of communicating the basis for such decisions to persons without specific training can often be a very difficult one. Of crucial importance, however, is a basic administrative problem. Most managements are organized around one or several key decision points from where orders are issued and carried out as a matter of directive by the organization. Is it feasible to complicate further the points at which decisions are made by introducing the union as an active party to such decisions? The success of such a venture in cooperation depends, in part, upon recognizing the organizational and administrative implications involved.

It is important to point out that the Studebaker Corporation and Local 5 have not engaged, as yet, in significant joint efforts to increase efficiency. The net result of their constructive relationship, however, may be greater efficiency than otherwise would have been the case. Studebaker management has been concerned with productivity. It must probably increase productivity to maintain or enhance its competitive position in the automotive industry. Because of the relationship it has enjoyed with its workers and union, the company will probably be able to secure union consideration of any measures appearing to be necessary to meet this objective. In a period of real crisis some program of outright union-management cooperation would be, perhaps, a logical outgrowth of the present relationship. Yet, the very existence of constructive union-management relations at Studebaker may itself be a factor preventing a future crisis on worker productivity.

Constructive union-company relations represent a stage of development out of which active cooperation on production problems can arise most easily. It is probably true that the "crisis" character of union-management cooperation is less pronounced where it springs from a situation in which a "problem-solving" approach to collective bargaining prevails. Nevertheless it is of crucial importance to recognize that cooperation to solve production problems is at best a relatively temporary stage of union-management relations. The underlying stable collaboration is found in the unspectacular, but more permanent, constructive union-management relations.

It seems apparent from what has been suggested in this chapter that constructive union-management relations require difficult and far-reaching adjustments in outlook, policy and practices for both union and management. Probably the most severe adjustments are made by the management officials. It is not an easy road to follow. Nor, once on the road, is progress necessarily rapid. The limitations on absolute sovereignty which arise out of union-management relations, even when recognized, may not be acceptable to the parties.

We have indicated some of the probable limits to the development of constructive union-company relations resulting from factors over which the company and union have no direct control. Implicit in this discussion are the equally important practical problems of developing this kind of labor-management relationship, granting that both parties desire that end.

IN SUMMARY

Our conclusion is that the greatest potential contribution of collective bargaining to the American economy will come through stable constructive union-management relations rather than through sporadic experimentation with spectacular types of union-management cooperation. Productive efficiency is an important managerial objective. A constructive union-management relationship can contribute toward that goal. Worker security is a primary concern of organized labor. Constructive relationships with management are an important means of achieving that goal. Through this kind of collective bargaining it may be possible for management and labor to harmonize the goals of economic security and economic progress while still retaining their functional independence in a democratic society.

In the mass production industries constructive relationships are likely to be most common in medium-sized and small concerns. As competition becomes keener for these concerns the development of such relations may be a necessary condition for the survival of the company and the continual employment of the union membership involved. Particularly will this probably be true if wage levels negotiated with the big corporations continue to be applied across the board throughout entire industries. But competitive forces cannot be counted upon to lead to constructive union-management relations in the power centers. The question of corporation survival and maintenance of employment is not so likely to be a determining factor in negotiations between organizations such as General Motors and the GM Department of the UAW. Negotiations between such giants do not conform solely to our economic environment; indeed they actually tend to create much of the economic environment for the mass production industries. As we have indicated, the forces influencing collective bargaining in the power centers make the development of constructive union-management relations difficult. Here lies the most crucial problem in present-day labor relations.

Index

Index

Addes, George, 26
Agreements: General Motors—UAW-CIO (1946), 91, 91n.; Studebaker—Local 5, 134-136, 155, 157-159, 167-168, 171n.; U.S. Steel—USA-CIO, 94, 95, (1947), 199-200
American Federation of Labor (AFL), 6, 7, 109, 122, 151, 187
Anderson, H. W., 90n.
Arbitration, 150-151
Automotive industry, 107n., 191-193, 198: conversion, 31-32; economic conditions, 18; General Motors, 15; pattern-setters in, 181; relation of Reuther group to, 27; social class differences in, 194; unemployment in, 18; wages, 137, 195

Bakke, E. Wight, 210, 210n.
Baltimore and Ohio Railroad, 215
Bean, A. G., 106
Berle, A. A., 4, 5, 5n.
Brown, Donaldson, 53n.

Carnegie-Illinois Steel Corporation, 199
Chrysler Corp., 11, 104, 107n., 181
Clothing trades industry, 192-193
Coal industry, 184n., 193
Collective bargaining: area of, 198, 200, General Motors—UAW, 67, 68, 75, 86, 87-88, 89, 90, 92-93, 97-98, General Motors view, 45-50, Studebaker—Local 5, 134, UAW view, 28, 29; industry-wide bargaining, 183; problem approach, 219, *see also* Studebaker—Local 5 relations; Studebaker—Local 5 concept, 141-146
Communist party, 26

Competition, economic, 5-6, 195
Conditions of employment, General Motors—UAW, 77-78
Congress of Industrial Organizations, 6, 7, 30n., 37, 122, 184, 187, 189n.: Industry-Council plan, 30n.-31n.
Constructive union-management relations, 10: advantages and problems, 212-214; channels of communication, 214; cooperation, 214, 217; defined, 202-203; differentiated from cooperation, 203; elements of, 204-208; foremen, 212-213; implications, 209-221; power centers, 211, 221; size, 210-211; stewards, 212-213; summary, 220-221; *see also* Studebaker—Local 5 relations
Contracts, *see* Agreements
Contract administration: General Motors—UAW, 78-79; in power centers, 186-187; *see also* Grievances, Umpire

Dewey, Thomas E., 55
Drucker, Peter F., 52, 52n.
Dymond, R. R., 216, 216n.

E-M-F Company, 109
Economic competition, 5, 6
Economic power: concentration of, 4, 5, 7; use of, General Motors, 74, General Motors—UAW, 22, 190-191, Studebaker, 132-133, 162, 176, 209, *see also* Strikes
Employment, full, 200
Erskine, A. R., 106, 109

Fact-finding Board, General Motors case (1946), 88-89, 91n.
Fairless, Benjamin, 94
Ford Motor Company, 11, 20, 96n.,

225

Ford Motor Company—*continued*
104, 107n., 181, 195: negotiations (1947), 95, 96, 96n.
Foreman's Association of America, 96n.
Foremen, 155: Studebaker, 161, 170, 173; under constructive union-management relations, 212-213

General Electric Company, 5, 8, 199
General Motors, 3-12, 15-100, 107n., 145, 181-201, 209, 211, 221: attitude toward labor legislation, 188; attitude toward UAW, 66-67; automotive industry, in, 15; competition within, 53; decentralization in, 52-53, 185; employee relations activities, 69-70; industrial relations policy, 23, 24-25, 27-29, weaknesses, 22-23; labor relations policy, 45-64; objectives, 54-58; pattern-setter, 10-11, 15-16, 104, 114, 130, 138, 181; size, 15; unionization of, 17, 19; *see also* General Motors—UAW relations, Management prerogatives, Power center, Strikes, Umpire, Wages
General Motors Department, UAW, *see* United Automobile Workers, CIO
General Motors—UAW relations, 3-12, 15-100, 181-201: agreement (1946), 91, 92n.; areas of agreement, 76-86; areas of disagreement, 73-76; attitudes (1937), 20-21; balance of power (1947), 96-97; collective bargaining, area of, *see* Collective bargaining; collective bargaining, issues, 72-100; contrasted with Studebaker—Local 5 relations, 176; corporation survival as factor, 221; economic power, use of, 22, 190-191; industry wide bargaining, 73-74; local level, 79-80; mutual understanding, 68; NWLB cases (1943-44), 33-34; negotiations (1947), 91-97, 188; negotiations and strike (1945-46), *see* Strikes; precedent approach, 98; public relations, 71-72, 142n.; scope of, 15; seniority, *see* Seniority; strikes, *see* Strikes; summarized, 97-100; union recognition, 20, 22; worker loyalty, 69-70; *see also* General Motors, Management prerogatives, UAW, Umpire, Wages

Golden, Clinton S., 215n.
Government intervention in industrial relations, 192-193
Government policy toward organization, 19
Gregory, William L., 126n.
Grievances, 199: General Motors—UAW, 80-85; power centers, 186-187; Studebaker, 144, 147, 152; Studebaker—Local 5, 123-124; *see also* Umpire, Contract administration

Hoffman, Paul G., 105, 106, 109, 112, 135, 137, 141-142, 148, 150, 174
Holmes, Oliver Wendell, 2
Hudson Motor Company, 107n.
Hupp, George C., 126n.

Incentive wage, *see* Wages
Industrial engineering, 161-163
Industrial peace, 103, 104, 132-133
Industrial relations: patterns, 100; purpose of research, 3-4; *see also* Constructive union-management relations, Labor-management relations
Industry-Council plan, 30n.-31n.
International Association of Machinists, 16n.

Job control: General Motors before unionization, 18; Local 5, 131-132, 169-170, 172, 178

Labor-management relations: effect of unionization, 190-201; *see also* Constructive union-management relations, Union-management relations
Lever Bros., Toronto, 216, 217, 218
Lewis, John L., 92, 193
Local 5, UAW—CIO, 3-12, 103-178, 202-221: as AFL local, 109, 122; community background, 117-121; community, relation to, 206; elections, 127; equity between members, 175; factionalism, 207; meetings, 125-126; membership control, 123-124, 167; officials, 126-127, 142, 143, 149, 150, 151, 154, 169; out-plant activities, 127-128; policy, economic uncertainty, 129-130; public relations, 156; status and power, 132-133; supervisory personnel, relation to, 126; UAW,

Local 5, UAW—CIO—*continued*
  relation to, 124-125, 150-151; *see also* Studebaker—Local 5 relations, Constructive Union-management relations, Job control, Union security

Management prerogatives: General Motors, 47-49, 51, 99; General Motors—UAW, 74, 89; Studebaker, 141, 153, 155-156, 167, 177; Studebaker—Local 5, attitudes toward, 135-136
Martin, Homer, 21, 22, 26
Means, Gardner C., 4, 5, 5n.
Mechanics Education Society of America, 16n.
Merritt, W. G., 90n., 91n.
Murray, Senator James E., 90n.
Murray, Philip, 30n., 36n., 95

Nathan Report, 189n.
Nathan, Robert N., Associates, 36n.
National Association of Manufacturers (NAM), 39n., 40n.
National Industrial Recovery Act (NIRA), 19
National Labor Relations Act (NLRA or Wagner Act), 19, 29, 56-57, 88
National Labor Relations Board (NLRB), 22, 26, 184: General Motors elections, 22, 184
National War Labor Board (NWLB or WLB), 33, 33n., 34, 44, 74, 78, 91, 138, 147, 199: General Motors cases (1943), 33
Naumkeag Steam Cotton, 214, 217
New Deal, 19, 56, 66, 188
Nyman, R. C., 215n.

Packard Motor Company, 107n.
Planning, 29, 30, 31, 32, 76, 99, 188, 191-193: advocated by UAW, 98-99; General Motors, 192
Power center, 11, 176, 183-189, 215: administration of contract, 186-187; automotive industry, 10, 11, 181; basic industries, 8; characteristics of labor-management relations, 183-189; constructive union-management relations, 10, 211, 221; cooperation, 187; defined, 181-182; effect on Studebaker, 205-206; free collective bargaining, 188-189; General Motors, 10, 17, 104, 181; pattern-

Power center—*continued*
  setting, 195n.; policy determination, 184-186; politics, 188; production efficiency, 193-194; size, effect of, 183-184; social class differences, 194; in steel, electrical manufacturing, meat packing, 10; wages, 195-196; *see also* General Motors, U. S. Steel
Problem approach, *see* Studebaker—Local 5 relations
Production efficiency, 193-194, 200

Reuther Group of UAW, 26-45, 72, 93, 94, 97, 192
Reuther, Victor G., 37n., 91n.
Reuther, Walter P., 16, 20n., 22, 26-45, 33n., 35n., 39n.-40n., 46, 67, 71, 84n., 86, 90, 90n., 91n., 95, 188, 196: attacked, 40, 67; on economic organization, 37-40, 39n., 40n.; *see also* Reuther group of UAW
Rochdale, 39n.
Roosevelt, Franklin D., 33
Ruttenberg, Harold J., 215n.

Safety committees, joint, steel, 199
Seniority, 32: General Motors, layoffs and rehiring, 24n.; General Motors—UAW, 76-77; Studebaker, 131, 160, 168-173, bumping, 158-159, 168-173; U. S. Steel, 199
Severance pay, 200
Sherman Act, 56
Sloan, Alfred P., Jr., 51, 51n., 52, 52n., 55, 55n., 56, 56n., 196, 196n.
Smaller War Plants Corporation, 5n.
Smith, E. D., 215n.
Social Security, 54-55, 200; *see also* Welfare plans
Steel industry, 187, 189, 192, 193, 194, 195; *see also* U. S. Steel
Stewards, Local 5, 155, 161, 164, 170, 173, 212-213
Strikes, 198: General Motors, sitdown (1936-37), 19-20, 23-24, (1939), 22, 184, (1945-46), 34-37, 67, 71, 86-91, 164, publicity in, 71-72; UAW proposed moratorium, 32; *see also* Economic power
Studebaker Corporation, 3-12, 103-178, 202-221: bargaining meeting, 170, 171; board of directors, 141-142, 143, 144; competitive position, 164; decision making, 142-

Studebaker Corporation—*continued*
143, 145-146; employee morale, 212; industrial relations department, 146; labor policy, 113-116, concessions at a price, 114-115, 174-175, 177, following the pattern, 114, security for union, 115-116; management organization, 110-111, 207; policy background, 104-113, continuity of management, 108-110, financial and competitive position, 105-108, problem approach, 111-113; public opinion poll on, 118-119, 122; size, 118; worker loyalty, 121, 206; *see also* Constructive union-management relations, Management prerogatives, Studebaker—Local 5 relations

Studebaker—Local 5, UAW, relations, 3-12, 103-178, 202-221: agreements, *see* Agreements; allotting new cars to employees, 173-175; attitudes and techniques of parties, 208; bargaining meetings, 154, 167; collective bargaining, area of, 134; company's competitive position, 205; concept of bargaining, 141-146; "not cooperation," 204; discipline, 166-168; economic power, use of, 132-133, 162, 176, 209; exclusion of outsiders, 150-151; features summarized, 204-209; grievances, *see* Grievances; issues, 104; meetings, minutes, 104n., 153-154; mutual trust, 147-148, 156-157; negotiations (1947), 168-169, 173; pattern follower, 205-206; policies summarized, 132-133; problem approach, 111-113, 141, 151-154, 163, 168-169, 176, 207-208, 219; procedural devices, 208-209; production problems, 219; publicity, 151; seniority, *see* Seniority; sharing information, 148-150; stability, 178; summary, 176-178; supervisory employees, 116, 126, 145; time study, 161-163; wages, *see* Wages; work standards, 160-162; worker loyalty, 206; *see also* Constructive union-management relations, Job control, Local 5, UAW—CIO, Management prerogatives, Seniority, Union security

Supervisory employees, 116, 126, 145, *see also* Foremen

Taft-Hartley Act, 97
Taylor, Senator Glen H., 90n.
Tennessee Valley Authority, 34, 39n.
Thomas, R. J., 21
Time study, 161-163
Truman, Harry S., 89

Umpire, impartial, General Motors —UAW, 27, 44, 47, 49, 60-61, 81-83, 199: General Motors attitude toward, 85; UAW attitude toward, 84-85
Union-busting, 28-29, 198
Union-management cooperation, 187, 214-219: defined, evaluated, 203-204; *see also* Constructive union-management relations
Union-management relations, 3-4: effect of fight for worker loyalty, 190; patterns, 176; in power centers, 183-189; status of parties, 198-199; *see also* Constructive union-management relations, Union-management cooperation
Union movement, 6, 7
Union security: General Motors, 74; Local 5, 116, 124, 135-136, 206-207; Studebaker policy, 115-116; Studebaker view, 205; UAW, 91
United Automobile Workers, AFL, 21-22
United Automobile, Aircraft and Agricultural Implement Workers of America, CIO (UAW-CIO), 3-12, 15-100, 103, 181-201: attitude toward General Motors, 66; Board of Review Committee, 81n.; demands, early, 24; demands (1943-44), 33-34; economic power, 182-183; executive board, 43, 43n., 81n.; factionalism, 21-22, 24, 26, 40-41; General Motors Department, 22, 27, 41-44, 60, 74, 80, 81, 81n., 86, 104, 185, 221, national council, 42, 43, negotiating committee, 42, relation to locals, 44, sub-councils, 42; locals, 45, 84, 185; objectives, 27-29; out-plant activities, 70; plans for war production and postwar reconversion, 29-32; public relations, 89; relation to Local 5, 124-125, 150-151; size, 16; strike, *see* Strikes; view of General Motors policies, 28-29
United Automobile Workers, Local 5, *see* Local 5, UAW

United Electrical, Radio, and Machine Workers of America (UE), CIO, 8, 16n., 93, 93n., 94, 95
United Mine Workers of America, AFL, 7, 184n., 193
United Rubber Workers of America, CIO, 93, 93n.
United States Steel Corporation, 5, 8, 11, 21, 94, 95, 182, 183, 185, 185n., 189, 193, 195, 199-200
United Steelworkers of America, CIO, 7, 8, 94, 95, 185, 187, 188, 199-200

Vance, H. S., 105, 106, 107, 109, 150

Wages: annual wage, guaranteed, 75-76, 92; automotive industry, 137, 195; General Motors, 86, 1946 contract, 89, 1947 negotiations, 92-95; General Motors—UAW, ability to pay, 88, 89, 90, 92, the 1947 negotiations, 93, wage-price controversy, 86-91; Lever Bros., Toronto, 215-216; negotiations, 1947,

Wages—*continued*
92-96; patterns, 138; power centers, 195-196; severance pay, 200; steel, 195; Studebaker, 130-131, 136-141, 147, incentive, 131, 131n., 137, 138-140, 163, and seniority, 171-172, inequities, 157, 164-166; U. S. Steel, inequities, 199
Wagner Act, *see* National Labor Relations Act
War Labor Board, *see* National War Labor Board
War Production Board, 31, 33
Welfare plans: Ford—UAW, pension, 96n.; General Motors—UAW, 75, 1947 negotiations, 92, 95; U. S. Steel, 94, 200
Westinghouse, Manufacturing Company, 94
White Motor Company, 106
Wilson, Charles E., 54n., 56n., 71, 84n., 88n.: on area of collective bargaining, 56-57; on social security, 54-55; on UAW, 50